FIERCE
Vulnerability

A Colored Girl's
Truths, Trials, and Triumphs

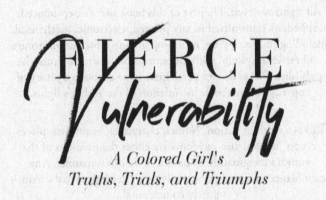

FIERCE
Vulnerability

A Colored Girl's
Truths, Trials, and Triumphs

SOPHIA J. CASEY

Tandem Light Press
950 Herrington Rd.
Suite C128
Lawrenceville, GA 30044

This is a work of fiction. Names, characters, businesses, places, events, locales, and incidents are either the products of the author's imagination or used in a fictitious manner. Any resemblance to actual persons, living or dead, or actual events is purely coincidental.

Tandem Light Press paperback edition August 2020

ISBN: 978-1-7353210-1-1
Library of Congress Control Number: 2020942664

PRINTED IN THE UNITED STATES OF AMERICA

To Josh, my sun son: thank you for the beacon of love and light that you are and for showing the world what fierce vulnerability looks like in human form. I love you.

"No eye has seen, no ear has heard, no mind has conceived what God has prepared for those who love Him."

—1 Corinthians 2:9 (NIV)

JEAN-MARIE

I T'S NO SURPRISE to see her take total command of this room. Most virgins to the game would be scared out of their minds on a night like this, but not the formidable Ava Whitman. We're all here to celebrate her candidacy for Mayor. This grandiose hall full of dignitaries and political bigwigs from all over DC struggles to contain her. She may be new to this scene, but she's damn sure done her homework. What she may lack in experience, she sure makes up for with ambition and sheer magnetism! I mean, damn! I give credit where credit's due; the woman practically oozes sex, power, and confidence. Tonight, she seems to glide as the silk fabric of her Armani suit brushes across her revealed thigh giving just a glimpse of her soft mocha skin. Her thick naturally wavy hair is sleekly drawn back to the nape of her neck in a bun perfectly showing her single-strand pearls. She has a no-nonsense look as the venue lights highlight her cheekbones. Her voice is both honey and fire as she claims her place in the mayoral race during her speech. Miss Ava is bringing allll the boys to the yard. Hah, poor babies. If they only had a clue as to who they were dealing with. While I'm excited for Ava, I must admit that I can't wait for this week and next week to be over. It's all I can do is think about packing for New York and that damn mammogram. I know today is super important for my girl though, so I'm glad I'm here.

I've known Ava since she was a stuck-up teen. Her sister Gladys and I became friends back in college, when we were freshmen together at West Virginia. We watched out for each other and became very close. For decades we were inseparable until Gladys was diagnosed with liver cancer a few years ago. After she passed, I took it upon myself to treat Ava as I would a little sister. Now, as a holistic wellness advocate, the other women in our circle tend to see me as a mentor figure, for better or worse!

"Jean-Marie, look at Ava over there getting it!" Vanessa whispers to me.

She and Ava go way back. They were college girls together at Spelman down in Atlanta. Vanessa has always been the flashiest of the group. Tonight her asymmetrical mauve dress graces one shoulder and plunges daringly below the other.

We share a knowing look and burst out laughing. Vanessa, myself, and Simone are having a ball over here on the sidelines at our table. As for Simone, she is the newest member of our gang. I met her at a networking event for female entrepreneurs almost a year ago. I was impressed by her brilliance and business acumen. She looks pretty in her royal blue caftan all sprinkled with shiny silver and gold threading. I love how Simone wears the most beautiful clothes but many times it seems extra for the occasion. She reminds me a lot of Phylicia Rashad with her buttery skin and chiseled features. For some reason though, she is clueless to her power often showing up in a room like she's apologizing or in the way or something. Then on the other end, she over does it as if trying to compete with Ava. It even shows up when she talks about her lackluster dating life. We can't go anywhere without men breaking their necks to gawk at her, yet she's always complaining about not having any real suitors or not knowing what the ones she does meet see in her.

Ava's campaign dinner is a verrrry formal affair, and so needless to say, we colored girls are here to show our love and liven things up a bit. That's what we're about!

Ava was seduced long ago by the world of power and political intrigues. She's extremely ambitious, always willing to get what she wants, regardless of the means. Her motto, just like her campaign slogan, is "Go hard or go home." She is careful to align herself with people who are strong and powerful. She holds herself to an extremely high bar and naturally holds everyone else to the same impossible standards. Now she's making waves all throughout DC as the one to watch for her mayoral campaign. She's really come a long way.

"I need to get in touch with her campaign manager," Simone is saying. "I've been wanting to make a contribution." Simone moved to DC from California after purchasing a local payroll business. Her intellect is more than a match for the job. She runs her fingers through her hair and adjusts her silver bangle.

I'm definitely the outlier of our group of chic, tailored executives. I wear my hair the way God gave it to me, big and wild, tamed at the moment by a soft scarf. My dress is loose and flowy with just a touch of cleavage—though it's hard to find a dress that can fully manage these babies! I like to think it's because I'm wiser but sometimes I think it's my way of exaggerating my confidence so I find a place where I am comfortable in my skin.

"We can hook you up later this week," I respond to

Simone in mock seriousness. "We wouldn't want to pull her away from the big dawgs tonight!"

"Hmmm…I wonder which one he is?" Simone muses, gazing intently at the cluster of suits hovering around Ava. I look over to share the man candy, just in time to see Ava moving in our direction.

"I can't stand these softy wannabes," she says, having just escaped a crowd of admirers. The girls and I collectively laugh and snicker. I can feel the energy in the room shift to our table and I automatically sit up a little straighter, trying to ignore the occasional flash from a photographer.

"Well Ava, if you're too overwhelmed, maybe I can take a few of them off your hands!" Simone giggles to herself. I look over at Ava just in time to catch her serving Simone some serious side eye.

"Uhh yeah, good looking out Simone. Those clowns definitely can't handle me, but who knows?" she says with high sarcasm. "Maybe they're more your speed." Oh boy. Ava never really did take to Simone. As the newest and youngest member of our group, she's still a bit wet behind the ears. Her sometimes delicate sensibility obviously rubs Ava the wrong way. I give Ava a dirty look.

"Well, WHATEVER!" I say, grabbing my champagne flute. "It's incredible to think of what four little brown girls are capable of, huh? We're out here baby! Doing aaaall the BIG DAMN THANGS! Cheers to the Colored Girls!" I look around the table and my eyes are met by a look of thanks from Simone. We clink our glasses and drink.

"Excuse me!" Vanessa rises from her seat, glass in hand and earrings flashing. "I just want to commend you for your tremendous success, Ava! You killed it tonight, with that speech. You are definitely an inspiration mama, congrats!"

Ava smirks. "Thanks babe! It's true I've been working on making this happen for a long time. It feels good to finally be recognized, I am SO ready to run this town!"

"Hello, may I borrow you for a while Ms. Whitman?" All heads at the table turn to greet the very tall and very sexy Clay DiNofrio, DC's own District Attorney. Now, Ava typically has no patience for most men, being a notorious ball buster. Consequently, her dating history (including her failed marriage) reads as a string of ego battles and power-plays, proving time and time again that she can out-man every man she meets. I've noticed that since her divorce, she's taken to dating inferior men to make herself feel powerful. Fortunately or unfortunately for her, DiNofrio seems like a whole different animal. Frankly, the way he was looking at her was making the whole lot of us jealous!

Ava smiles a wolfish "game-on" smile.

"Hmm, I think I can spare a moment." She gives us a wink before walking off with the sexiest man in the room.

"Damn!" Vanessa says. At the very same moment I received a text from Ava.

Don't wait up ;)

I laugh and share the message with the other two. "Ha, don't have to tell me twice! I have a crazy day ahead tomorrow, just on my way out."

Vanessa says, "Sounds good to me." Simone begins to gather her things. "Ahem!" Vanessa clears her throat dramatically. "Ladies, are we still on for our spa day on Friday? Because I have us booked at Fountain Day Spa!"

"Ahhhh yes, definitely! See you then!" I am looking forward to this! I will need a little R&R before my trip to New

York. I sigh, take one last look at the glamourous scene before me, smile and head out.

~❦~

By Friday morning I am all packed and ready for my training in New York City. As I began to lock up my suitcase, I feel the warm hands of my husband Stephen slide around my waist.

"It's that time already, eh?" he asks, kissing me softly on my neck.

"Yes sir, it's about that time! Just gonna take my things out to the car, then I'll be out of your hair until Monday morning."

"Baby, aren't you headed to the spa beforehand? Why don't I take you over now, and I'll bring your things to you, once you're done? I can take you to your bus after."

I don't know why, but I resist taking him up on his offer. I like doing things for myself…that way I can be certain it will happen, or if it doesn't, I won't have anybody to be disappointed in but myself. But I meet Stephen's eyes and see a genuine light in them, and accept his offer.

Upon arrival I wait just inside the doors for Ava, Vanessa and Simone. I close my eyes and take a deep breath, reveling in the soft music and the soothing lavender scent.

This is exactly what I need right now. It's hard to believe the state of my life. There's so much to be grateful for. I admire my sumptuous surroundings. It's like the staff here know exactly what I like. The sweet, soothing smells of lavender and jasmine oils, the sound of the water trickling over the stones in the quaint coy pound, and the soft music playing all instantly calm me. This is Vanessa's favorite spa. That girl's taste is dead right. I see Simone entering through the double doors, her heels clicking smartly against the tiled entry. She smiles warmly at me.

"Hi Jean, I hope you weren't waiting here too long." I assure her I haven't been. She smiles again shyly as she fidgets with her keys. "I'm really glad we've been able to connect more."

It seems like there is something weighing on her mind. "Me too! I'm glad we met." I smile back, and hold her gaze. Her brown eyes soften, and she seems to find peace within herself. We relax into a comfortable silence.

"You know, it's meant so much that you all took me into your little group. It can be kinda hard to meet folks when you're new to town. I really appreciate it."

Simone is so genuine and sweet, it sometimes catches me off guard. I chuckle, "Simone, we're so happy to have you! I know we've only started really getting to know each other, but it seems like it's been ages to me." I watch her eyes light up.

"That's how I feel!" she exclaims. "Although I know Ava's not too sure about me yet." She looks anxiously towards the entrance.

Well, I'm not one to sugarcoat things. "I know Ava can be a little abrasive at times. She holds herself to near impossible standards, and has been through so much, Simone.

She's definitely got a chip on her shoulder about a few things...don't take it personally. I think it's easier for her to project her insecurities onto others sometimes...You know what I mean?"

"Yeah, I definitely get it," Simone smiles meekly at me, before excusing herself to the ladies' room.

I hear a commotion outside the front doors, and turn to see Miss Vanessa parading towards us. Ooh Vanessa with her dutiful hubby Michael in tow, looks like a page fresh out of a beach resort travel magazine. Her tan linen wide-legged pants and matching sheer scarf blow lightly as Michael closes the door. Vanessa, a darling of the home décor industry, can always be counted on to be up on all the latest trends, be it fashion, wellness, or parenting. She and Michael, a congenial white doctor, have four gorgeous children. She prides herself on rubbing elbows with the upper echelon and keeping up appearances at all times. After all, what else would you expect from a Southern belle?

"Hi there Jean-Marie!" she gushes.

Her overtures are met with a dramatic eye roll. "Oh HEY girl!" I muse mockingly as she kisses my cheek. After all, it's twenty minutes past the time we were set to meet.

"So sorry to keep you waiting, Jean," says Michael, looking frazzled and distracted. I've always liked Michael. His temperament is so precise and clinical, such a picture of the typical doctor. We are both earn a living from healing others, but our approaches are on such different ends of the spectrum that we often end up ribbing each other when East clashes with West. He thinks I'm some sort of witchdoctor, and I'll own it.

"Yes, we were just out trying to button up some details for the twins' birthday bash! It's going to be amazing. We are so excited, right baby?" Vanessa smiles into Michael's eyes as she smooths his already-smooth collar. "Alright now, you have a surgery to get to at Sibley Memorial, don't you?" she croons.

"Yep," he replies. "It's one of those more experimental procedures so I'm not sure when I'll be home."

"Perfect. I should be finished here by one, and I'll have the nanny come by to pick me up." Vanessa sighs, dramatically. "Ah, my prince." She and Michael share a chaste kiss before he bolts to the car.

Vanessa fusses with her weave. "By the way, Ava is bailing for today. She's at an impromptu press conference downtown.

I still can't believe everything is happening so fast for her!" I hear her footsteps before noticing Simone's reflection in Vanessa's Gucci sunglasses.

"Oh! Hi, Vanessa, you look amazing."

Vanessa gives Simone a quick look over, chuckling and giving her best polite smile. "Ah, Simone! I wasn't sure if you were coming today." She adds hesitantly, "You look nice, don't you feel a bit over-dressed?"

Simone laughs half-heartedly and shrugs her shoulders, "I had some business in the office this morning."

I close my eyes and shake my head. I mean yes, Simone does seem to try a little too hard at times, but Vanessa didn't need to point it out. It's a bit strange to notice how hard she tries to fit in with us. After all, she's newly wealthy, brilliant, young and gorgeous.

Vanessa heads to the front desk to check us in before we walk over to the changing rooms. I suddenly find myself feeling a little nervous. Everywhere I look are wealthy women in great shape, shamelessly walking around nude or in very little clothing.

"Heaven help me," I murmur to myself while trying to scope out a private corner to change in. I begin making my way to a secluded area before I hear Vanessa's voice.

"Hey Jean! I found three open lockers altogether over here, c'mon!"

"Great!" I lie. I definitely prefer undressing in private. Shedding my clothes here makes me feel so far out of my element. As I remove my dress, I notice an older white woman watching me. She fixes me with a frosty gaze that says, "How'd YOU get in here?" I do my best to ignore her and change as quickly as possible. Stealing a glance at Vanessa, I realize she'd lost quite a bit of weight. She's always been attractive, and now her body is trim and fit. She is even showing off a bit. Obviously Vanessa was in no great hurry to find her towel. She strode around, casually nude and obviously comfortable. I look over at Simone. She too is quite lovely. *What an amazing figure*, I think to myself. I can't understand why she is changing so modestly. Like me, she is doing her best to keep herself covered up.

"Ah, I love this place! I try to make it here once a week," says Vanessa. "Let's get started in the sauna!"

"Wow, I confess I've never been to a spa before!" Simone said as the three of us entered the steam room.

"What?" Vanessa replied in mock shock. "Simone, you haven't lived! This is an absolute necessity for women like us. Isn't that right, Jean?"

I smirk in response. Naturally this type of treatment was wonderful, but it certainly wasn't something I did for myself every day! To be honest, I hadn't been to the spa in years! It's not that I can't afford to, it's just never been a priority of mine. Though Stephen and I pull in plenty of money, I always feel tight-laced around my spending, and so busy! There's something in me that deems this kind of thing a bit too frivolous to do often. Maybe it was a sense that if I overindulged, it would take the sweetness out of the experience. The sauna is unbearably hot at first, but in time my body adapts to the heat. As much as I want to relax, I just can't seem to. My mind, as usual, is on overdrive with thoughts around Stephen and the kids, my budding holistic wellness practice, and my looming mammogram just around the corner.

"Jean-Marie, hello?" Simone had been trying to get my attention.

"Oh, sorry, just off in la-la land I guess."

She laughs and points to a snoring Vanessa. "Hmm, apparently you're not the only one."

"Now that's one for the books!" I say. There is Mrs. Vanessa Wescott, the proud socialite, head knocked back, mouth wide open, snoring and murmuring quietly in the corner. I giggle and automatically reach for my cell phone to snap a picture, then remember that it is stowed away in my locker and Vanessa's pride is safe for now.

"I've been meaning to ask you Jean, how is your healing practice going?"

"Oh, it's going great!" I reply, a little too fast and a little too chipper. Simone looks at me a bit questioningly.

"Great, I'm glad it's going well." She could take a hint. The truth is, I feel a little insecure about my practice right now. Obviously that wasn't anything I would ever share though, especially with Simone. I knew how much she admired me, and there was no way I could tell her how conflicted I've been feeling.

"Actually, I almost have too many clients right now! Business is really taking off, just the way I knew it would!" I hoped she bought it. "What's been going on with you?"

Simone sighed. "You know Jean? I really can't complain. I'm in good health, my finances are on point. Daniel is finishing up his senior year and trying to decide between Georgetown and Harvard—you can guess which school I'm rooting for. Feeling blessed to be rolling with you ladies here in DC. It's just that something is missing. It'd be so nice to have a man in my life, you know? I got so used to Daniel being the little man around the house, but he's grown now and just about to leave. I mean I know I can handle myself, but I just feel lonely sometimes."

I just gape at her. I don't know what it is about Simone.

Sometimes I can't believe how vulnerable and candid she is. It could make me pretty uncomfortable at times. She is too raw for her own good.

"Well, have you been putting yourself out there more, in the dating world?" I ask, trying to be supportive.

"Sure. I mean, I go out to events to try and meet men. Often I'll start conversations with guys I find attractive, but it never seems to pan out. It's confusing. I hear all the time that I'm such a great catch, but I can't seem to hold a man's interest past date two!" I can hear the pain in Simone's voice and don't know quite what to say.

"How are you and Stephen doing?" Simone changes the subject.

"Oh, Simone, we're great. He's such a wonderful man." I consider leaving it at that, but I decide to divulge a bit more. "Sometimes I wish we could connect a little more. It's always been so hard for me to accept support from others. I've been hurt and disappointed so many times in the past. Yet somehow I found this incredible person who genuinely wants to love and support me. He really challenges me to trust and let go…It's scary sometimes, I have fear that he'll let me down like others have before. He is so consistent with how he spoils me, yet I find myself questioning it all. I know it's my issue though, he's never given me reason to distrust his intentions… I have to really check myself, sometimes I'm tempted to push him away…do things myself. I dunno. He's just so supportive of me, and even though we've been married for three years, sometimes it's still hard for me to put all my faith in him. At the same time, I love and need him."

I think about just how much I will need him in the next few weeks. My annual mammogram is just around the corner, and for some reason I've been extremely anxious about it. Just a heavy dread surrounding it that I can't shake. I don't feel like sharing about that just yet though. I'm a little surprised to have opened up as much as I did about my insecurities.

Simone looks thoughtful, and lays quietly for a while before asking how I find wellness clients in the area. I am lost for a reply. Truthfully, I know what there is to be said, but I am embarrassed to admit that I am not in a place to market for clients in the local area. I serve most of my clientele through webinars and trainings online. It provides just enough distance for me to feel comfortable. Who am I to coach folks in areas of life where I myself was blocked? There have been times when I felt like a fraud, teaching others how to heal their bodies while neglecting my own. We sit silently as I craft my reply.

Vanessa wakes with a start and almost loses her towel. I bite my lip, trying not to have too much fun over her indignity. She proudly lifts her chin up and pretends to have been listening the entire time. I turn slightly away from Simone, relieved for the interruption.

We leave the steam room, helping ourselves to the complimentary champagne before taking a small dip in the pool.

"Mmmm, that feels good," says Vanessa. "I needed this after the crazy morning I just had!"

"Oh yeah, what's happening?" I ask her. She lets her head roll back and lets out a long sigh. Apparently she is having issues with the petting zoo that is providing the ponies for the extravagant event she is throwing for her twin boys' birthday.

"It has to be perfect. My boys always have the best, and this party will be no different!" I fail to hide a smile, and laugh outright. She makes a face at me.

"Nessa, your boys are three! I'm sure they will be thrilled

by the Superhero impersonators, chocolate fountain and candy buffet. Why are you killing yourself over this?"

She gives me a curious look. It seems the answer to my question is one she dare not acknowledge, especially out loud. So she simply continues on the same tangent. She goes on for a while. I think about engaging her again, but it is just about time for me to leave. I say my goodbyes to Simone and Vanessa, ease into the protection of my dress with a feeling of relief, and switch gears mentally in preparation for the weekend ahead of me.

Of course, Stephen is right on time. I can't say how much it means to see him there, as promised, with all my luggage and Jason rearing to go in the back seat. Jason is my youngest, a handsome little nine-year-old man, but I somehow still see him as my baby. I have a daughter too, Maria, who is hanging out at a friend's house.

"Hey baby!" I rain kisses down all over Jason's giggling face. "Aaaah! Mommy stop, stop! We've gotta make your bus! Let's go!"

I look up to meet Stephen's gaze. He's got that bemused, contemplative look again. I want to tell him how much this means, but I opt for a thigh slap and a wink instead. "Let's get this show on the road, shall we?"

On the way to the bus, Jason asks questions about my weekend away. My heart lifts as I sense his childlike concern for me. I reassure him that I will be safe by myself in the city, and try to explain more about the training that I will be attending.

Stephen drives along quietly. He truly is a rarity, this man of mine. He is so steady and consistent, so simple in his desires. Handsome in his way, bewilderingly out of his element in society, but with a warm sense of humor at home.

The CIA couldn't have found a better man to manage part of their intelligence analytics. And, somehow, he adores me. I shift in my seat.

I receive a text from Ava. "Call me tonight, will you?" I tell her I'll get back to her as soon as I'm settled in my hotel. We reach the bus stop and Stephen gathers up my things. I say good-bye to my boys, holding my husband tightly but looking away. Now it's time to board the bus to New York City.

As we pull into Port Authority I feel myself go into autopilot. I'm so familiar with my routine now, when I'm in the city. Hail a cab to the hotel, order room service, unpack my things...I call Stephen to let him know I got here safely. Then I dial Ava.

"Giiiiiirl!" she exclaims.

I laugh, "Oh it's like that, huh Miss Ava?" Ava tells me about her flirtation with Clay. They have a date tomorrow night...and she's trying to play it cool, but I can tell she's excited. It's good to see her feeling confident enough in herself to take a chance with a powerful man.

"Ha, we'll see, Jean-Marie. I'm not looking to get my panties in a twist just yet! I'm all about qualifying a man first, you feel me?"

I snicker dramatically. "Is that why you've been single as ever for three years?! Oooh got 'em!" I laugh. I like to come heavy with Ava, since I know she can take it.

"Hmmm, quite frankly Jean, I can handle mine. The older I get, the more I realize I really don't need a man. All the things I really need, I'm more than capable of doing for myself! Hell, I have bigger balls than most of these dudes out here." She punctuated herself with a hearty laugh. She might have fooled another friend or acquaintance, but not me. Her words wrung a bit hollow. However well I knew her, above all else, she would never admit her real feelings. Not even to me.

"Mmhmm," I mused. As much as I loved talking to Ava, I had to cut it short. This weekend's training would no doubt be as demanding as it's ever been, and I could not afford to lose a good night's rest. "Well whatever Ava, I'm excited for you! I've gotta run, but I want to hear all the dirty details on Monday!"

She laughs and blows a kiss through the phone. I hang up and shake my head with a smile. Tomorrow night will be very interesting…

❧

I wake up with just enough time to shower, dress and grab a hasty cup of coffee before we begin. I've missed out on the group yoga session, but then it's not the first time. I get a lot of energy from attending these trainings and conventions. It's a big part of why I do what I do. I get to help others heal in a natural way, being true to themselves, and there is always something new to learn. I know that I'm earthy crunchy, and for some people that's a bit of a turn-off. But I've also seen many people turn to me when conventional medicine fails them and they have opened up to other methods.

As I head to our meeting room, my phone vibrates. It's Stephen texting me pictures of him and the kids making goofy faces. *I love that man!* I think to myself. I admit though I just don't get how he turned out to be such an amazing father and husband seeing as his upbringing was completely crazy. His parents both being addicts and Stephen bouncing around from foster home to foster home. *There must be a God.*

I walk into the training room and see several of my holistic wellness colleagues posting up their goals for this session. My friend Allison is there, tall and gorgeous, tossing her blonde hair to the side as she writes in her goal with a black sharpie.

"Allison, honey!" I greet her with a quick hug. We haven't spent much time together outside the classroom, but I have always felt a nearness to this white young thang. We keep each other awake during the afternoon sessions, often with quirky irreverence.

"Hi Jean-Marie! I'm so glad you're here. You can use my sharpie."

I realize the focus of the morning session will be intimacy. I turn towards the goal board, my mind sorting through what I might truly need this weekend. I scan some of the other goals to get my bearings: Continue to date my husband, even though we're married. Find the confidence to open up about my past. Learn how to tell my kids I love them.

"Oh, Lawd, give me strength," I mutter to myself, placing the sharpie back on the table and taking my seat next to Allison.

This field I've chosen is a strange one. Most professions are very linear, like Stephen's—he goes to the office every morning, receives data, provides analysis, makes an output. Now, there are variables and meetings and people to deal with, but his process is direct and quantifiable. My business is the human body, and most often, the mind and soul. It's a subtle science, one that our culture often rushes past in a busy unawareness. Our trainings are usually a mix of Eastern medicine and personal development techniques to help us really reach our clients.

This morning we spend a great deal of focus on vulnerability and our personal blocks to it. The idea is that if we as practitioners cannot open up and be willing to be exposed, our clients will sense our reluctance and mirror it. I recognize that I refused to post a breakthrough goal for this training session, and I begin to search my mind for the cause of my hesitation. Intimacy. For some reason I feel a well of anxiety bubbling up within me. That's the sensation I always get when I am on the verge of taking new ground. I find myself slowly tearing small shreds into the paper in my lap.

Suddenly there is something for me around claiming myself fully as a holistic wellness advocate—not just a mentor but a force of light and transformation on this planet. It's a strange sensation, as if an entire flood of thought enters my mind at once, unbidden and external. In my mind I can see myself helping others face-to-face, I can see healing and light transforming their lives and then radiating to others. I see myself as powerful and impactful, a state of being that I don't yet recognize in myself, but one that I know in that moment is flawlessly true. I am nearly overwhelmed by the sense that this greatness will flow into the lives of those who I love.

I feel that some time has passed when I gain awareness of my surroundings again. The trainer is leading the audience through a writing exercise, and I realize that my paper has fallen to the floor. I blink several times and become conscious of the tears streaming down my face. *They're going to think I'm off my nut,* I think to myself as I gather my things and make a beeline for the door.

I find the ladies' room, push in, then close my eyes and breathe deeply. I am grateful to be alone, for the safety of this space. I walk over to the sink, rinse off my cheeks and stare at my reflection in the mirror. It's the same Jean-Marie, my wild, dark curls flying, my voluptuous body concealed by a flowing skirt and billowing scarves. Have I been hiding? Am I hiding now? Who was that powerful person that I saw? My brown eyes look back at me, staring me down with a clarity that seems to contain a challenge.

I feel a sudden anxiety and stop myself from seeking the refuge of one of the stalls. Instead I face my reflection and consciously breathe through my fears. I can hear the outside corridor begin to fill with people and realize that the session is over and my solitude will not last long. I leave the restroom, a weak smile plastered on my face as I search for a quiet corner of the hotel. I need to think. I find a small, empty sitting area tucked into a corner and collapse into one of its chairs.

Power huh? It's true, I've made great strides in my life. Could it be that I'm finally ready to claim my power, and allow myself to be the leader I have always been below the surface? I can't help but think on all the times in my past when I felt powerless.

My mind turns back to my childhood, that little brown girl in a mess of siblings, often feeling lonely even in the crowd. I know I was loved in a way, but I learned early to mask any emotion that would upset the fragile peace—fear, anxiety, a feeling of smallness, lack of control. Power? Not a chance. Any vulnerability was scorned, so I pushed any emotion deep down inside myself, swallowing it whole.

I can feel my thoughts going down a darker path, and in panic I fight it will all my being. *Not here,* I think to myself, shaking my head and willing my mind to focus elsewhere.

But the images and thoughts are unstoppable. My mind turns to New Orleans, my childhood home. The stillness of dark nights, listening to the silence with every nerve of my body, holding my breath and willing my heart to stop racing and wishing I could vanish into the night. The sounds of the others sleeping, the cicadas humming in the darkness. It didn't happen every night, but the anxiety haunted me constantly.

Finally, dreadfully, the creaking of floorboards outside my door. I recollect the tight feeling of desperation invoked by that hollow sound, and my body echoes that feeling. I begin to tremble.

The door opens without a sound. Well-oiled. I squeeze my eyes tight shut, willing myself to find escape in sleep or death, as I feel him standing over me, his breathing hushed but ragged. Hands, strong hands, hands that should have been my protectors. I can feel the warm roughness of those hands, sliding over my skin, pulling my gown up and lingering over my budding breasts. The hands slip my panties down to my knees, and I hold my breath against the pain. The mattress springs groan under the added weight as he sinks into me. Tears wet the pillow as I tremble in pain and silence. The scent of his sweat, the motion and the breathing are so unforgettable that I can taste them now. Sometimes he would lie next to me and sob silently before leaving the room. And then I would curl up as tight as I could and pretend to vanish.

Mental, physical, emotional anguish. The sun would rise in the morning, and everyone would make nice, going through the movements but avoiding my eyes. Denial. My only protection was in silence. I was never heard.

I am shaking, my face buried in my hands, silent sobs raking through my body. I am furious with myself for allowing this to happen here in this open space, and the fury fuels the emotion coursing through me.

I feel a tentative hand on my shoulder, and a soft voice says, "Jean-Marie."

I freeze, closing my eyes tightly. Here we go. I peek up through my hands, and the concerned blue eyes staring down at me register as my friend Allison's. Safety. I slowly release my breath and find myself melting into her arms, sobbing quietly until I am spent. I try to collect myself.

"You must think I'm craaaazy," I whisper, not yet trusting my voice. I straighten and look around for a tissue. Allison passes me a bottle of water from her bag, maintaining contact with my arm with her other hand. "You don't have any peanut M&M's in there, do you?" I joke, trying to lighten things up.

"It's okay," she says gently. "Do you want to talk about it? You must have been triggered by something today."

I find myself opening up to this woman in a way that I have never allowed myself open up to anyone. There are times that I stumble for the right words, but the fear is missing. She has already seen me so raw...what's the point of hiding anymore? Something happens to me as I hear my own voice owning my story. I feel courage, support. Power? How can there be power in this humiliation? But I can't deny that it's there. Power, strength, courage, and hope.

Allison watches me intently, listening. I can feel her supportive energy, and there are times when she brushes away her tears. I finish my story, and we sit in stillness for a time.

"I think you're on the right track," Allison says. "You're getting a sense for who you want to be, what you want to become, and that can be scary. You are preparing to move forward so powerfully that your old story wants to hold you back, wants to reassert itself. You old story is comfortable. Painful and flawed, but it has been yours for a long, long time. It can feel threatened by the new story you are now creating for your future.

Maybe you needed to relive the pain one last time, so you could release your past and begin to embrace something new."

I can feel the truth in her words. I feel a renewal and a new sense of determination. Perfect the future will not be—but

I'm ready to begin. I feel inspired to journal about the things that I've learned this afternoon. I don't want to have to learn them again. And I realize I'm starving.

"Whew, that was some heavy stuff, girl. Thanks for hearing me," I say, a little timidly. "Well, it's too early for a drink, which is what I really need. That or chocolate. Definitely chocolate."

We find a pastry shop just down the street and barely make our afternoon session.

❦

It's been a long, emotional day. I am spent as I make my journey home. I doze off in the cab to Port Authority only to be woken by an alert on my cell. I check my voicemails and am greeted with the joyful sound of my Jason singing a silly song. My heart swells for that boy. I laugh loudly, and see the cabby watching me curiously in his mirror. I could care less! I am tired, happy and so ready to be heading home. The cabby watches my smile fade as I listen to the confirmation call my doctor left me. I'll be taking my mammogram three days from now…I immediately feel a sinking feeling in my gut.

❦

I had agreed to meet Simone for lunch just before my exam. It seemed like a good idea at the time, but I've felt so anxious this morning that I wonder if I'll be able to focus. I roll my eyes and shake my head at myself. Ridiculous. It's not like this is my first mammogram. I know the drill. After some time, she walks in to the deli looking sullen and distracted.

"Hey Simone! What's going on lady?" She smiles a little smile and comes back at me with a generic reply. "Not much,

I'm fine. How are you?" she asks, although I can tell she's hardly paying attention.

Before I answer her, I see her brighten. "I told you my Daniel is days away from graduation?! He's so busy with end-of-school events and formalities, he's hardly getting any sleep. I think he's made up his mind about Yale, which is good, it's a great school, though I'll miss him. It's hard Jean, I want to spend as much time with him as possible, but of course he'd rather spend his time with his friends. I considered throwing him a party, but I think that would only cramp his style."

There was something going on with Simone for sure. Of course, having your only child graduate from high school was emotionally taxing, but I could tell there was something else weighing on her mind. Her neat pantsuit couldn't disguise her eyes—she looked as if she hadn't slept for nights on end. It was easy to see she was ambling through her own secluded world of worry. I press her again.

"What else is happening with you?" Ever polite, she smiles weakly before asking me about myself. I really couldn't believe it. Here was Simone, the most genuine and candid woman I'd met in a long time, and now suddenly, she was withering on me.

"How was your training?" she asks all too quickly, her quiet desperation growing in volume, eager to stop my probing.

Sighing, I look out the window at the flurry of cars going by. "I'm choosing to open myself up. I'm giving myself per-mission to lead the most powerful life I can. I got so clear this weekend, Simone. The impact I dream of having on the people in my life is impossible unless I claim responsibility for my own experience...I'm beginning to understand that it starts with me, and really that's perfect. It means the future I want to create for my communities and loved ones cannot come together without my best self. It cannot work any other way. So the first step, is to start with me."

I look into her eyes just then, and witness something unexpected. I see some nameless thing come undone in Simone. Her breathing has slowed, she seems newly present and open. I speak not a word. We sit softly in silence for some time. Hesitant, I chance asking, "Did something resonate?"

Her smiling eyes meet mine again as swift tears come. But too quickly she is wiping them away, staunching the natural free flow down her lovely face.

"Gosh Jean-Marie. I don't know what this is…I don't know why I'm reacting like this." Shamefully she closes up again, looking small and far away. That sullen look returns as she composes herself. "Actually…I'm so sorry Jean-Marie, but I have to go. We'll talk soon, okay?" She scrambles for her things, and with fresh streaming tears, hurries out.

I wonder at the complexity of that woman, wonder what twisted hurt she had gotten so close to sharing. I wonder at the secret joy and passion she'd hidden away. Maybe I should follow her, press her for more? No, I smile to myself, realizing everything had happened just as it needed to. I felt as if something magical had just opened up between us. There was a space created in the midst of our shared guardedness—a lightness and rare visibility felt. Although it felt risky to share myself as I had, at first, I now felt more grounded in my own skin than I had in a long, long time. Maybe I'd created a breakthrough in authentic communication. I know I was in process, but I was pretty sure that the sudden openness she experienced briefly was triggered by my willingness to be open with her. I laughed aloud. The very thing I had been trained in this last weekend, and here I was experiencing it firsthand for the first time. I was eager to practice and develop this with my clients.

I finish my sandwich and stare at the clock. It is almost time for my appointment. I feel the now-familiar sinking in my stomach. I tuned out, onto autopilot then, paid my bill, and in a fog somehow drove myself to the hospital.

In the waiting room I thumb through *Home Journal* magazine and find an article about Vanessa. As usual, she looked tasteful and stylish in the editorial. The interview high-lighted her "seamless" work-life balance, illustrated by the glossy photos of her, Michael and the kids. Her new home was well-manicured, clean and picturesque. *Living the dream*, I think to myself.

"Mrs. Chandler?" a shrewd-looking nurse calls out to me. I smile and follow her to the examination room.

I take a deep breath to calm myself. Disrobing, I fol-lowed the familiar instructions. The metal feels cold and cruel against my body. I cringe and try to take my mind off the dis-comfort. This screening seems to take longer than I remember, so I am extremely grateful once it's over. The technicians are all very sweet, and ensure me I will have results within a few days. I thank them and head home to my family.

"Mamaaaaaa!" Jason screams, hurling himself at me like a mini superhero. I hold him to me. "Okay, okay!" he says, trying to squirm away from my embrace. I keep hold of him, my precious boy.

"Do I get some, too?" Stephen asks, standing in the threshold with a mischievous look. I finally release my son and look at Stephen. He wraps his arms around me, and sways us side to side. I let my mind race, and do my best to keep myself from looking him in the eye. I haven't found the space to tell him about my breakthrough weekend, or even that I had just had an exam. Something in me wants to break. Wants to let myself relax and let myself remember the feeling of his arms supporting me, holding me up.

"Hmm?" I pretend not to have heard his question. I kiss his nose and break free towards the kitchen, messing with Jason's little fro as I pass, eliciting boyish squeals of indignation. I can feel Stephen's eyes on me.

I know I let myself get wrapped up in my son. With him it's so easy to show my love. At the end of the day, he depends on me…I never worry that he'll let me down. I know I'm doing it again, deflecting Stephen's attention with Jason, but I put it out of my mind now.

My daughter, Marie, is in the kitchen making cookies. "Hi, Mama," she greets me and we talk about her day. She is just finishing up her first year of middle school, fiery, brilliant and disorganized. She's got a fierce mouth, and it sometimes gets her into trouble. She's my little hellion. Sometimes we butt heads, and lately I've had to back off a little to help her embrace her independence.

We make dinner and finish homework. I busy myself with voice and emails, while Stephen helps the kids wash up and prep for bed.

By now they're done. I hear their "goodnights" down the hall, and turn on the TV in our bedroom. He enters the room and raises his eye at the television. I laugh aloud at whatever programming is on. Stephen slips into bed and I kiss his cheek. I turn the TV off and talk fast about an early morning meeting. He sighs and looks deeply into my eyes so that I feel he sees straight through me. He simply kisses me softly, issues a, "Good night, Marie," turns and sinks his head into this pillow.

Damn this man! I think crazily to myself. I want very

badly to tell him about my mammogram, and the anxiety that's been weighing down on me. I want to cry and let him hold me, and yet…I look over at my sweet husband. I watch him for a long time before turning over, my eyes wide and glistening with tears in the darkness. Why do I feel the need to be strong on my own? Why do I keep him at arm's length? I let the tears pool down the side of my face, collecting on my soft, downy pillow. I begin to drift off, then I feel Stephen's arm around me. I smile.

SIMONE

I GLANCE AT MY phone and see the faint blue glow: 12:48. My eyes focus for a moment on the light of the background picture. The handsome three-year-old in swim trunks gives me a hint of a smile, even through the weariness. I close my eyes again and sigh, trying to sink deeper into my silky sheets. My body is exhausted, but my mind is churning out thoughts furiously. I consider about taking another Ambien but I don't think it'll help. I shift my body and give in to my thoughts.

Tomorrow morning—no, in just a few hours, I think grimly—*I have some meetings with the attorneys*. I turn the situation over in my mind, considering if there is anything else that I can do to prepare for it, and decide that there is nothing more I can do. I have been so consumed with worry and fear that I wearily dismiss it.

I consider my disastrous lunch date with Jean today. There was a moment when I thought I might tell her everything, but I decided to keep it in. The women out here in DC are different than in the West. So strong, so determined. I know they aren't perfect, but they feel the need to act as if they are, and when I try to share with someone, I often feel their disdain. I don't want to lose Jean-Marie's respect. I can wait. Once this whole thing blows over, I know the deep shame that I feel will leave me.

Daniel has an awards ceremony tomorrow in the evening, followed by his graduation formalities and all-night senior party the next day. He has been such a trooper these past few weeks, working hard on his final projects and exams. It hasn't been easy for him to move out here to DC, switching schools at the beginning of his junior year, but he threw himself into schoolwork and lacrosse and made the most of it.

He misses his old friends though. I consider what his life would have looked like had we stayed in San Diego. In retrospect, it seems like it was a sunny, simple life, but I know there were difficult times, especially in the beginningand in the end. The life of a single mother is never easy.

I was just finishing up my MBA at the University of San Diego when the pregnancy test came back positive. I could feel my entire universe completely halt for just a moment, I remember it being the oddest sensation. I had just began a "casual" relationship with a guy, and the results were anything but. I didn't even tell him, I just stopped returning his calls. I didn't tell anyone. But my focus was completely gone, and I finished my finals by the skin of my teeth to earn my degree.

The pregnancy was rough. A couple of days after graduation I became so ill that I couldn't keep anything down and a roommate drove me to the hospital. The intake nurse was the first person who I told. I ended up staying there for a couple of weeks, hooked to an IV so I could get the nourishment that my body was rejecting. That first day in the hospital, everything came crashing down for me. My lease was expiring, so I needed to move my things out of my off-campus apartment.

I was scheduled to start an internship in the executive office of a manufacturing company the following week. My future had been so open, so clear and full of promise, and now I was unsure of everything.

I knew I had options. I knew other girls who had gotten procedures done and moved on with their lives. Since my illness was a symptom of my pregnancy, I would be able to get right back on my feet. There were times when a termination felt like the best decision, even the right decision. What would become of me otherwise? Did I have the strength to do this? To be a mother? The real question, the one that kept staring me in the face every time I thought I had made the decision, was could I live with myself if I went through with it?

I called Mom from my hospital bed, still unsure of what I was going to say. My parents are religious and traditional, so I knew this was going to be hard for them. She talked and cried with me as she drove straight to the hospital, and then held me like a baby for a long time. Dad came for a visit, and I held my breath as he walked into the room, but he simply sat down beside me and quietly asked what he could do to help. I had never felt such love before, or since.

My parents were right by my side as I swept up the pieces of my life. Dad moved my things and took care of the apartment. I called my supervisor and declined the internship, citing medical problems. Mom was right by my side until I was well enough to leave the hospital, and then she took a sabbatical from work so she could continue to help me. I moved back home, right back to the same old suburban neighborhood I grew up in, after six years of being away.

They were there in the hospital when I brought my Daniel into the world. I was so afraid that day, so many different fears, fear of the future and what kind of a life I could offer my baby boy. I took one look at his squishy face, with his little scruff of black hair, and felt a palatable wave of intense love wash over me. He was here, he was mine, and in that moment I knew everything would work out as it should.

With the help of my parents, I built a good life for the two of us and a solid executive career for myself. I dated from time to time, but I'll admit that I had lost confidence in my ability to develop a healthy relationship with a man. Love seemed so serious all of the sudden, so heavy. I didn't have much time for romance, anyway.

Then one night three years ago, my parents were driving home on the 405 and were hit head-on by a drunk driver who had gotten on the onramp going in the wrong direction. They passed instantly, and everything changed for me. My entire support system had vanished in the night. I dealt as best I could with the funeral arrangements, the estate, and with a very messy criminal case. After months of grief, anxiety and loneliness, I decided that I needed to get away—to pick up and start all over, somewhere completely new. So I sold everything, cashed out my savings and my inheritance, and took a chance on a payroll business in DC that looked promising.

"Promising," I snort aloud into the silence, surprising myself. It was anything but. I shake my head and roll over. My mind is finally slowing down, and I gratefully drift into a deep sleep.

❧

The elevator opens to the third floor of the building that houses the offices of Ingenuity Payroll Services. My heels click past the reception area as I walk towards the executive offices, past the vast room of empty cubicles. In another hour the place will be humming, but for now the desks are dark. I stop and lean over the top of a pod of cubicles, ruminating about the lives of those who work here and the consequences today will have for them. I try not to think about the emptiness that might become permanent and move on to my office.

I switch on my computer and answer a few emails. The truth is, things were looking very promising for my small company when I came in two years ago. The previous owner had gone into retirement and sold at a reasonable price. Our earnings were strong, and our reputation for being the best local payroll processing service was pristine. Growth was slow and steady, and though the team was not perfect, we were always able to fulfil our contracts.

Several months ago, Henry, the controller, came to me with some disturbing trends. We were slowly bleeding money, and for all of our searching through records and bank report audits, we could not isolate the leak. Month after month the gap between our available funds and our commitments grew, and now things were at a breaking point.

So far I had kept the information very close. Only Henry, myself, and the attorney that we kept on retainer were aware of the situation. But I knew now that I was in over my head, and I had hired a team of consultants, an attorney and a forensic accountant, to come in and help.

At stake? The Health Savings Account balances for tens of thousands of local families. If we went under, they would have no access to the funds that they had contributed. It would be a disaster for the DC area. I close my eyes and breathe deliberately to clear my head. "You got this, Simone," I tell myself. I can't afford to lose my composure now.

I have a few anxious minutes to kill before the meeting, so I navigate over to a local news site. A picture of Ava Whitman alongside her opponent for mayor flashes across the screen.

It looks like the mayoral race will be a tight one. I study the two faces, vastly different in almost every respect. Her white male opponent, Brad Thompson, has a cold look about him. My eyes linger on Ava's arched brow and the intensity of her gaze. I try to breathe in some of her confidence.

My thoughts snap back to the present when the speakerphone comes to life. "The consultants are here," the receptionist's voice announces. I straighten my jacket a little shakily, pick up Henry from his office, and lead the way to the reception area.

"Hello, I'm Simone Orchard," I say, extending my hand to the two suits in reception. I am completely disarmed for half a second by the first set of eyes to meet mine, warm and hazel with a touch of brilliant green.

"Maxwell Ellis, I'm your forensic accountant." Tall, slender, bronze skin against white teeth. *Oh my* I think.

"Good to meet you Maxwell," I say, a little too quickly. I shake hands with Jonathan, the consulting attorney, and hastily regain my composure. "Thank you both for coming." I smile towards Henry and he shakes their hands.

This is Henry, the Controller here at Ingenuity. Please follow me back to the conference room and we'll get started."

I turn and as we make our way, I remind myself that *I am Simone Orchard, MBA, owner and CEO of my own business in Washington, DC I am tough, confident, and my head is clear. I may be surrounded by suits and testosterone, but there isn't one of them who has worked harder against all odds to be here than me. A woman of color does not gain the position of power that I have by accident.* But in the back of my mind I am also berating myself for letting my guard down. I will not allow myself to become captivated and lose my clarity over a well-fitted suit. I raise my chin a little higher as I walk.

We enter the room and take our seats. Henry prepares his files, and I switch on the computer to start my presentation. Breathing through my fears, I intentionally plant my feet and square my shoulders. "Gentlemen, let's get started." My voice is commanding and strong, and I am determined to make equal eye contact with everyone in the room. I don't care how good he looks in that damn suit.

✧

I am looking forward to tonight. It's Daniel's final high school awards ceremony, something exciting and normal after the chaos at work. My Danny has gone on ahead with a friend, looking so sharp in a new sport coat with a bright green tie that he insisted on tying himself. Lately I can feel him push me farther away. I know that he is simply preparing to claim his independence, and I'm grateful for that. He is going to do just fine on his own. But all the same my own response is to try to pull him closer, to keep him near me as long as I can. I don't like to think about it, but I know it's part of the reason he chose an out-of-state school. He needs to find himself, outside of me. I'm just not sure what my life will look like when I am left to myself.

As I drive to the ceremony I allow images of Maxwell Ellis to fill my mind. I'm feeling hopeful after our discussions today. My consultants are sharp and have some good theories. *Dear Lord, let it be enough*, I breathe. I feel like I may have been a little cold and impersonal today, but I was able to maintain my presence and leadership, so I'll count it as a win.

I park in the auditorium parking lot, pull down the vanity mirror and freshen up my lipstick. A sleek black Audi A6 pulls into the spot next to mine. I pull open my door and my eyes meet those of the formidable Ava Whitman in all of her polished glory, stepping out of the passenger seat of the A6. I glance down for a moment and take a breath before exiting my car.

"Hi there Ava!" I say, pulling her in for a quick hug.

"Simone!" she quips back. "How are things, girl? Of course you know this is Clay DiNofrio, District Attorney of DC." She gestures to her companion making his way around the car and we shake hands. "Clay, this is my...friend Simone Orchard."

I ignore her slight hesitation and greet Clay. It's no surprise to hear her dismissal. Ava seems to collect people like trophies, surrounding herself with only the most polished and powerful. She's made it clear throughout our relationship that she has no use for me. The night has taken a very awkward turn.

"I had completely forgotten that your son went to National Cathedral," Ava is saying as she slips her hand around Clay's arm. "What was his name again?"

"Daniel," I remind her with a small smile as we walk to the entrance. "And your Timothy is graduating tomorrow, too. I can't believe how time has flown."

"Yes well, things have been so busy for me," she retorts, her eyes scanning the crowd of people at the entrance. "Clay, I see the Fosters up ahead," she says discreetly. "Let's go say hello. I'll be seeing you, Simone?"

"Bye, Ava," I respond to the back of her head and watch her make her way through the crowd, causing a little stir herself. Looks to me like Ava Whitman, mayoral candidate for the District of Columbia, is becoming a novelty even among the exclusive, powerful parents who can afford to send their kids to National Cathedral. I allow the press of people to engulf me before finding a seat.

The ceremony is long and loud. I alternate between smiles and tears as I observe these young adults claim their achievements. My hands ache from clapping as I watch my own Daniel stand with a select group and receive his academic awards, along with a few scholarships. Tears steam down my cheeks and I have to put my hand to my heart.

I meet Daniel outside afterwards and hold him tight to me. Even in heels, I have to raise my chin over his shoulder. "I'm so proud of you, baby." My voice catches in my throat.

"Mom," he says, pulling out of my embrace. "Some of the guys and I are going out to get some food. Don't wait up for me, okay?."

I see a group forming nearby, including a girl who has her eyes on Daniel. "Have a good time," I say as he joins them, and stop myself from asking him to text me if he is going to be out later than 1:00. In just a few months he is going to be completely on his own, and though it hurts, I need to take a step back.

JEAN-MARIE

I AGREED TO MEET Ava for a drink after work at Echelon, an upscale lounge spot we're in the habit of visiting every so often. My eyes adjust to the darker lighting scheme of the top floor amidst the buzz of people chatting and laughing. It's easy to find Ava. As usual, there is a cluster of men hovering around—a sight so commonplace it begins to feel like part of her outfit choice. Although the place caters to a younger clientele, we normally have no problem fitting in. The poor young guys lounging close by can't seem to place Ava's age, only noticing a fit body and fly style under the dim pink lights. As usual, she seems much more interested in the contents of her glass than the admiring eyes surrounding her. She orders another just as she sees me walking her way.

For a moment her cool demeanor is broken by an impish little smirk. I laugh outright, surveying the thirsty-looking pack of boys and join her at the booth.

"What's up sis? What kind of riff-raff are you getting into now, hmm?" I laugh and order a specialty cocktail. Swinging her arm around the shoulder of the booth, she grins and takes a long swig of the whiskey concoction in hand.

"GIRL," she gives me a bemused look. "Now I know that you know I don't have time for these men out here, but I'm about to see what's happening with ma dude Mr. DiNofrio…" She looks me in the eye and laughs at my dramatic look of shock.

"Um yeah, I knew that was a done deal as soon as he whisked you away at your party that night!"

She scoffs. "I mean he's not ALL that Jean-Marie!" She fussed with her drink as a tiny smile threatened to ruin her glowering. "Anyway you know how I do…maybe I'll just break myself off a piece and tell him to keep it moving! He doesn't need to get his head all swoll up just because I've decided to give him the time of day…"

I shake my head and sample my drink. "No thank you! Miss Ava has no interest in getting all fussy over one fine man." I looked at her pointedly. "What? I can at least admit the man is fine!" She looks slightly annoyed, before downing the rest of her whiskey.

"Anyway Miss Jeanie what's going on in your world, hmm?"

I smile into my glass and savor its contents. "Not much girl, we missed you at the spa. As usual Princess Nessa made us wait so long we almost lost our appointment reservations."

Ava rolls her eyes. "I can't for the life of me understand why that women wants to blow a king's ransom on a toddler birthday party! Ain't nobody got time for that! Hell, my boys are lucky if I remember their birthdays! They don't want me around much anymore anyway, they'd rather be with their friends. Getting too big for their britches. Timmy just walked last weekend, all done with high school. He's got the grades but he won't commit to college. Says he needs some time to figure things out…looks to me like he just wants to keep living at home where the rent is free and he's close to his girl. Not sure what to do about that boy. And you know, Marlin's no help. I'm too busy with the campaign to worry about it anyway…"

I let her ramble awhile about her campaign. Ava is my favorite person to talk to when I want to take my mind off my own problems. She never seems all too concerned about anyone else, she never pushes—so she's the perfect person to escape into. She highlights the success she's been having on her campaign so far. I smile and nod, although her bravado comes on a bit too strong. The woman loves to come across as a battle-axe, but I can sense more of her just underneath the surface. We drink and titter away the time, laughing and cracking wise, people watching and chatting about the minor details of our lives. Before I know it, it's well past 11:00.

"Girl, let's get outta here," I say, giggling, as I reach for my purse.

"You go ahead Jean, I think I'll have another," she says, eyeing a fresh cocktail sent over by an older gentleman. I snicker and make my way out into the hot night …

Waiting on my taxi, I see a gaggle of young women in tiny dresses smoking and laughing outside. I watch them eye me curiously before my car rolls up. I feel the alcohol running its course through me, making me feel warm and tingly. Sleepily I watch my city roll by in the humid night. Paying my fare I get out and gaze awhile through the dark at my silent house. In my stupor, it seems somehow sad and self-loathing. Slowly I make my way up the little steps. The porch light temporarily blinds me, its accusatory glare hot and disorienting.

Once inside, I sluggishly make my way up the winding staircase, past Jason and Marie's dark rooms. A shy sliver of light peaks through a slit in the master bedroom door frame.

I enter to find Stephen, huddled and stooped over the edge of the bed, a crumpled letter in hand. He gives me a sad, resigned look. I stand my ground, feeling the heaviness in the air between us. He lays the letter on the bed before me.

"Why didn't you say something?" he whispers. Panicking, I realize he received my test results. The initial mammogram came back showing a lump. On that paper is my doctor's recommendation that I make some decisions on next steps of a biopsy.

"I don't know Stephen…I wasn't sure yet, so I didn't want to get you involved until I could wrap my head around this."

"Guess what Jean-Marie? I'M YOUR HUSBAND! IT'S MY GODDAMN JOB TO BE

INVOLVED! I'm so tired of this!!! Why won't you let me in? This isn't partnership! I always feel like I'm at arm's length with you. Like you can't trust me…Do you know what that's like? I would do ANYTHING for you Jean-Marie!!!"

I take in this man, tears streaming, breath ragged. Before I know it, I feel my own burning tears staining my face. I fall down on the bed and surrender to the torrent of emotions rushing through me. A desperate sob tears through me, unwarranted. I'm remembering all the men in my life who taught me not to trust. The ones who showed me always to keep my most precious, vulnerable pieces in reserve. The living evidence of deceit, incompetence and brokenness. I sob, raging against the sad and stubborn beliefs that run my life.

We remain distant awhile, each crying for ourselves, before we can come together. Stephen brings me a tissue and gathers me up in a fierce embrace. I taste the bitter saltiness of his tears as they mingle with mine. We are kissing and crying, slowly breathing, gently touching. Softly caressing now, fast falling asleep in each other's arms.

Morning comes. I wake to Stephen prepping for his work day. I begin my early routine. As I do my hair and makeup Stephen enfolds me from behind. Gently he kisses me on the cheek, and meets my shy eyes in the mirror. We watch each other's reflections.

"I love you, Jean-Marie," he sighs as he retreats. "You've just got to let me in, okay? Otherwise I don't know how to support you." He gives my hand a gentle squeeze before turning away.

I feel his words burrowing into my skin.

⁓

I awake with a start to my phone buzzing on the nightstand. My mind automatically turns to panic as I start imagining emergencies that might prompt a phone call at this hour. I grab the phone and answer as I find my feet and leave the room, hoping I haven't woken Stephen.

I hear rustling and incoherent mumblings at first, before I hear Ava's brassy laughter ringing in my ears. I tear the phone away from my ear, lowering the volume before listening to the rest of her message. Her voice sounds strange…drunk, I realize.

"HEY JEAN GURL! Hope all's tight and sexy with you mama, haaah…I was just calling to say hey, you know? Hey… girl, I just want to thank you, you know? Thank you for all your support, I really appreciate you believing in me. Cuz us bad bitches have to stick together, am I right? Yesss maame. Mhmm and you know it hasn't been easy girl. It feels like everyone is playing dirty you know? Everyone is looking at me, like I ain't shit…like I'm nobody out here." Her voice fades away.

"Ava, honey, where are you? Sounds like you've had one

too many. Do you need something? Do you want me to get you a cab?" I venture, though I'm guessing she's too far gone to know what she needs.

"Awwwh, no, Jeanie. I'm just fiiine. I just been drinking, you know, at home, and I was thinking about you," she slurs and I hear a clinking sound. "I really miss you, Gladys."

I pause, unsure of what to say. Gladys has been gone for almost three years. I feel the familiar ache in my soul when I think about her, and I silently mourn for Ava. I know my words won't truly reach her, not in her current condition anyway.

"I miss you too," I say, my voice cracking a little. "I miss you every day, little sista. Here's what I want you to do. Go into the kitchen and get yourself a glass of water."

I patiently talk her through a quick routine to get her safely into bed as I sit in the darkness at the top of the stairs. Eventually we say goodnight, and she calls me Gladys right up until the very end. My throat is dry and I know my eyes will be swollen in the morning from my silent crying. Gladys was a gift. She had a way of seeing right into you and understanding what you needed most to be your best self. She had seen me in college, seen me when most people saw an obese girl.

And she had seen Ava, seen her through the neglect of their childhood years, seen through her thorny exterior and found beauty in her soul. One of the first questions that I have for God when I meet him, is why He took Gladys away. Ava and I haven't talked about her in months. It is just too painful, still. I roll my eyes and pull myself up to my feet remembering that I have to get up to be at Vanessa's. Silly girl. It takes her getting fall-down drunk to be able to talk about something real. And she won't even remember it in the morning.

My alarm clock wakes me up a few hours later. I snooze

it and turn over to cuddle Stephen. I love the way his hair smells. Before I can doze off for a few more minutes, the alarm sounds again. What seemed like seconds was actually fifteen minutes later.

I drive through the affluent neighborhood, using my phone's GPS to find Vanessa's new home. I wonder at the posh, gated homes, reflecting on wealthy lifestyle of those within. "Ain't nobody in here mowing their own lawns," I mutter to myself, shaking my head.

As I pull up to the gate, Nessa comes out to greet me in a custom-made apron, covered in flour. I laugh at her as she leads me inside, noticing the beauty of the immense front entry and the trappings of wealth. "How must it be," I smile and sigh, allowing myself to be a little envious of the spotless space. But soon I realize how cold and sterile the house feels, despite the immaculate interior.

Nessa explains that she's been playing with dessert recipes for the birthday party. "I think I've found just the right recipe for eclairs to complement the cake. You'll have to help me taste them later. It's been so difficult coming up with the perfect desserts while keeping myself fit," she goes on theatrically, hands on her trim hips. "Everything tastes so sweet to me. How do you feel about a Waldorf salad for lunch? The maid has all the ingredients ready to go, we just need to put them together."

We settle into the kitchen and each prepare our own salads as Nessa continues to chatter away. It becomes apparent that Vanessa has a definite new obsession with her health. She has seemed to bounce back to her slim figure after each of her three pregnancies, but this is an entire new level of concern for her appearance. I can see her eye my salad portions as we sit down to eat with our glasses of fruit-flavored water. What must she think of me?

"Well honey, you sure seem to have your act together," I smile broadly and nod my head. "Mhmm. The typical American dream. Gorgeous home, doctor husband bowing to your every whim, four beautiful babies. You could be the poster child for everything a little brown girl could want to become."

Nessa raises her chin and gives me a satisfied smile, though I detect something incongruous in her eye. "Yes, it is a good life. Things are going so well for Michael at the surgery at Sibley, I wouldn't be surprised if he just keeps moving up that ladder.

The girls are loving their school, and the twins are out right now with the nanny. I honestly don't know how you do it without a nanny. With work and all of my other projects, I just don't see how you'd get anything done."

"Oh, we make it work. My little people are already through those tough younger years," I retort. We enjoy the rest of our food and chat a bit more about our children.

"So, are you going to show me around?"

Nessa shows off her home with a brief tour, including a look at her new home office. I notice how she carefully avoids any spaces that are not immaculate. She finally leads me back into the dining room.

"Have you heard from Ava lately?" I nervously finger the rim of my glass, waiting for her reply. Vanessa eyes me curiously. "I did see her just last week, why do you ask?"

I take a long sip of my water. "She called me last night, and I'm pretty sure she was blitzed."

Nessa laughs, "Oh, you know Ava, the girl just likes a good night cap every now and then, that's all."

I look at her awhile. "I don't know Nessa, I'm a little worried about her. I feel like the campaign is starting to take its toll. I know that it's no cake walk. I saw an article last week that was completely defaming, it really infuriated me. It delved right into her single parent childhood, her divorce, even her sexual life. All laid out for people to read and criticize. As if others are better, or don't have any of their own laundry to air. As if any of that truly has anything to do with the job description. Anyway, it can't be easy on her."

Nessa plays with her water seemingly deep in thought. We sit in silence for a while.

"I'm sure Ava is just fine. She's definitely the fiercest, most ambitious woman I've ever met. She always manages to get whatever she's after, sooner or later. I wouldn't worry about her too much." She snickers. "I, on the other hand, get overwhelmed so easily. I mean, this party is really stressing me out. Half of the vendors have been having issues, Michael's been so consumed with work. He barely has time to help with the party, let alone spend any quality time with me. At least I know the kids will have a nice time. I have a few magazines coming over to do an editorial on it too. Everything has to be perfect." She takes a long swig of her drink and chances a look at me. "Oh, I'm sorry Jean! I ran my mouth for a minute there, didn't I? Really I can't complain, everything is going pretty great at the end of the day."

I smile, although I can't shake the feeling that there is more underneath the surface of Nessa's words. I promise to send her some lavender essential oil to help relieve her stress. We finish our lunch and share some mindless gossip before I get myself together to leave. Nessa escorts me out to the front gate. I smile and wave as I get into my car to head out, but by that time, Nessa has already turned her attention elsewhere.

VANESSA

I WATCH JEAN-MARIE DRIVE away out of the corner of my eye, pretending to busy myself with a floral arrangement in the entry and suddenly feeling small and lonely in this giant new house. I tell myself that it's better that she'd gone when she had. Jean-Marie had a way of making me say more than I meant to. I wonder if it is because of this new training she'd started. "But she sure has become a busy-body, huh?" I think aloud to myself. *Why is she trying so hard to be in everybody's business?* I think as I stop myself from too many questions. I try not to ask too much, especially of my closest friends. There are certain things that one just shouldn't talk about.

I've known Jean long enough to see a change in her. Oh, she's always been overweight, and forever draping herself in layers and even the occasional African head wrap. I think she might fancy herself as a witchdoctor, I giggle to myself. Definitely non-conventional. She is easy to be friends with, though. Her laugh in infectious, and I never feel like it's aimed at me. There is an acceptance in her that makes me feel comfortable and it draws me in. I know she has been going to some soft skills trainings lately and they seem to be enhancing her natural abilities.

"Maybe I need me some relationship training," I laugh dryly to myself, finishing off my second glass of Merlot.

This party has got to be perfect. I feel so many eyes on me. Though I can't say that the kids will even appreciate it, they're so young now. Even so I feel it's the least I can do for them. They live in a world where status and appearances are very important. I can tell you first hand, it's not easy to be brought up in a mixed-race household. Especially in the circles we run in. It's as though as a mixed-race child you're still considered Black. I can't even bring myself to imagine my children going through what my siblings and I had to endure, especially my brothers. They were always being pulled over by the police for some reason or the other, never with a real cause. I sometimes think about what impact that had on them. My brothers always seemed angry—like ticking timebombs. I hated living through that life. I hated even the smell of our neighborhood in East St. Louis. My kids will not go through that bullshit. All the overwhelm and stress of making sure they have the best becomes worth it somehow, when I know they can hold up their heads and not live in fear.

I check the clock and mentally prepare myself for my oldest to come home from school. Sometimes I just don't understand what my kids want from me. My twin boys are pretty easy to please, mostly loud, and they still need their mama. But my girls are another thing altogether. Miranda is sixteen and Samantha just turned eight. I keep a beautiful home, make good money—enough to keep them in trendy clothes and gadgets—but they seem so far away at the end of the day. I don't know why I feel so awkward around them. I guess I just don't know how to be.

A key turns swiftly in the lock, as my eldest daughter Miranda saunters into the foyer. I pretend to busy myself in the kitchen, although that proves to be unnecessary. My moody daughter is already ignoring me, earbuds blasting, as she grabs a snack from the counter before bounding up the steps to her room. Not even a hello, no acknowledgement at all for me. I laugh aloud to myself. I guess I was avoiding her too.

I pass by her room on the way to mine. The door is shut, barely containing the loud, explicit radio music now dominating the second floor completely. I chance a quiet knock. The more seconds go by, the sillier I feel, as there's no way she can hear me through the sonic wall she's built around herself. I steel myself and throw all my weight behind a knock that would surely shake it out of its frame. Suddenly the door is flung wide open, my lovely and apathetic-looking sixteen-year-old blandly staring at me. I know my nervous smile betrays me and she smirks in reply, the look on her face quizzical and irritated.

"Mom, what's up?" I can barely make her out over the deafening sound ripping through her speakers. I make a motion for her to lower the volume, which she does begrudgingly.

"How was your day, sweetie?" I ask, wondering why it is I feel so nervous when I talk to her. Sighing, she looks around distractedly.

"Fine. Uhhh you?" My heart races a bit as I try my best to look nonchalant and relaxed.

"It was good! I just met with Jean-Marie, putting the final touches on the twins' party. It was, uh, pretty chill!"

Why did I have to say "chill"? Miranda, I could tell, was doing her best not to laugh out loud. "Okay, just wanted to check in, see you in a bit. Dinner will be ready at seven."

"Great," she replies before shutting the door. Not even halfway down the corridor, the house is once again ringing with abrasive rap music. I want to ask her to turn it down, but I also don't want to disturb the decent interaction we've just had. I know no one will be home for a while. The other kids have afterschool activities, and who knew what time Michael would be getting in. I collapse onto my bed.

Michael. I knew I should be happy about his recent promotion. He's wanted it for a long time, but now I feel like I barely see him. I am at a complete loss with him. Every time I try to talk to him, it feels like he becomes more and more distant. Honestly it seems to happen with everyone I try to get close to. I lay here for a long while, trying to let Miranda's loud music drown out the sadness that threatens to envelop me. Eventually though, it takes hold.

I find myself waking with a start later. I put my fingers to my aching temples, head to the bathroom, and down a painkiller before freshening up. Downstairs I greet the kids over the drone of the movie they are watching, and dismiss the nanny for the night. I bake lemon pepper chicken and asparagus for dinner and set out the dishes. After peeking out the window for Michael's car and finding the driveway empty, I call the kids in for dinner. The room fills with noise and little bodies as they pour into the space, and Julius begins to whine about the asparagus, poking it with his fork.

My phone buzzes in my pocket and Michael's laughing face flashes across the screen. He's going to be late for dinner, so sorry, it's just that he can't get away from some critical patients. No, thanks, don't hold dinner, it may be some time before he can come home. I hang up, feeling a wave of despair come over me.

As I place the phone back on the table, the faces of my

children come back into focus. Julius is smashing his asparagus into a green pulp, and Samantha has retrieved a box of macaroni and cheese from the pantry and is firing up the stove. I hear Miranda talking on her phone in the next room.

I escape back to my room with another Arnold Palmer and fall asleep before Michael gets home.

❦

My eyes adjust to the bright morning light. I awake alone in my bed, although the empty space beside me remembers my husband's body heat. I roll over onto the warm patch where he slept, feeling the sensation on my breasts. I soak up every last drop, the rare evidence I could scrape up these days that I was indeed sharing my life with someone.

Stretching, I survey the view from the newly-installed French windows. I take in the morning softness of the gated community with its rolling hills and designer cars. Soon enough I find my eyes have re-focused and all I can see is the sun glinting on the hard water spots on the window. I can see Michael's car is still in the driveway.

Quickly I put my hair up, throw on a robe and hurry downstairs, hoping to catch him on his way to work. I find him already finishing his morning coffee. Seeing me, he laughs into his cell, wrapping up with whomever he's been speaking to at this early hour.

"Hi baby," he delivers a swift kiss to my cheek. I smile an automatic smile.

"Who was that?" I ask, trying my best not to let my tone betray the negative feelings heating up within me. He studies me as he sips his coffee.

"Oh I was just catching up with Marlin, thinking about

taking a little fishing trip out on the lake with a few buddies for his birthday next month."

"Wow, Marlin, as in Ava's ex, Marlin?" He quickly finishes his cup.

"Yep! He's working in my wing now. Over the past few months we've become friendly I guess." Michael tosses his cup in the dishwasher, and briskly kisses my cheek before waving himself out the door.

I watch his car take off down the driveway, for once thankful to hear the kids waking upstairs.

⁓

That night I call him for the third time.

"Nessa." I jump. Although I'd been trying to reach him, the sudden sound of my own name startles me. "Hello?"

"Hi, love. When will you be home for dinner?"

"Oh, babe, I have a pretty intense wrap-up tonight. I think I should be home by 9:30, sorry for the late notice." A small sigh inaudibly passes my lips.

"Oh no, that's fine love, take your time." I entertain a small smile, although no one is there to see it.

"See you," he says. My smile widens, even as my disappointment deepens. I hang up and begin to feel a small knot weaving tightly in my chest. I make my way to the kitchen to fix myself a drink.

As usual, the young ones lay transfixed by their iPads in the living room. Miranda finishes filling her plate, already on the move to her bedroom.

"Honey?" I call to her retreating back. Slowly she turns to me, a look of bemusement and slight irritation snagged on her pretty young face. "Can you watch your siblings down here for an hour?" Anxiously, I wait for her to respond.

She blinks, staring dully. "I can't, Mom, I have homework to finish." I chuckle to myself dryly as I watch her retreating back once more ascending to the solitude of her room.

"Of course, dear!" Of course. I so desperately want some time to myself before Michael gets home.

Luckily, I can keep a fairly good eye on the babies as I finish the skinny cocktail. I savor the first bitter taste burning my lips and throat, unlocking something inside me, loosening the tightness I'd been carrying around all day. I luxuriate in the second sip.

Closing my eyes, I imagine all the small worries of the day falling away from me. I didn't realize it, but I nodded off for what I thought was a few minutes. *Oh my God*, I thought. *The kids!* I had nodded for almost a half hour. I freaked out rushing to the kids to just in time to hear something shatter.

The high-pitched wailing of one of the twins rips through my kitchen, tightening the knot of anxiety just removed. Hurtling over the child safety gate, I find Julian crying over one of my crystal figurines, shattered irreparably. I curse loudly as I hear Michael's key in the door.

Hastily I pull the flailing child in my lap, wordlessly checking for cuts and scratches.

"Oh nooo, what happened here?" Michael asks, slowly taking off his shoes and hanging his coat. Blood, hot and quick, rushes to my face. I hate him to see me this way. My eyes dart around the room, briefly forgetting the raucous baby in my lap, as I remember my unfinished cocktail on the counter, praying it will go unnoticed.

"Julian destroyed one of my figurines is all," I smile, trying to collect myself. Michael surveys the scene distractedly, his gaze settling on my cocktail. He sighs heavily as his eyes meet mine. I turn all my attention to little Julian, smiling broadly, crooning to him. When I look up again, I can only hear his mumblings and footsteps in the kitchen.

With Julius on my hip and Marcus in tow, I prepare them for bed. As they drift off, I sit atop the stairs. Through the banister I watch Michael mill about our spacious kitchen. He ravenously consumes handfuls of snack foods and desserts, never once checking the fridge for the wholesome meal he knew I'd made. I watch him polish off my drink. I then watch him smile and chuckle through what looked an awful lot like a ten p.m. texting session. Already, I could feel my imagination going into overdrive.

"Love, come to bed!" my voice cracks as I call over the railing. "In a minute," he replies.

Shaking slightly, I wrap my hair and prepare for bed. Slipping into a sexy satin chemise set, I get under the covers and wait, once again unsure of what to do or say. I lay there a long time for Michael. Finally, just before nodding off, the soft bedroom light comes on. I pretend to sleep as he prepares for bed, my mind caught somewhere between sleep and desperation. Through my closed eyelids I see the light vanish and feel the gentle shift of the mattress as he sighs into bed. For a moment my heartbeat seems to grow louder and more frantic. I turn my head towards him and raise my hand hesitantly, pausing just before coming into contact with his shoulder. I breathe, touch him lightly and whisper, "Baby."

"Hmmm?" he responds, shifting his body towards mine.

I wordlessly draw one leg towards him, separating his legs and bringing my knee between them. I move my body closer.

"I don't think so, baby," he says softly, his arms around me in a firm embrace. "Not tonight. I'm so exhausted from work. And frankly I'm a little worried about you. You're home alone so often these days while I'm working late. I know that handling the kids at night by yourself can be a burden, and I know it's not exactly your forte." He pauses, shifting and then looks me in the eyes. "You know how I feel about you drinking alone, especially when you are the only one here with the kids."

His arms suddenly feel heavy around me, as if his embrace is more like a scold. I silently stretch my legs back together and set my mouth tightly. I daren't speak. He sighs and loosens his hold on me.

"It's not entirely your fault. It's just that I can't be in two places at once. It's okay to know your limitations," he soothes. "You do so much around here with your work, the house, the kids. I think maybe the best thing for our family right now would be to hire some more childcare help to be here at night. Then you can focus on your work and your projects, do what you do best, and the kids will have the attention they need."

I freeze as his words sting me, and then I can feel my body relaxing as I go limp. I can feel the clinical accuracy of his words as I consider my role as a mother—the disrespect, the distractions, the drinking, the sheer imperfection of it all. There is a horrible sort of freedom in admitting to myself my failures.

"Maybe you're right," I say hollowly. "I'll call the agency tomorrow and see who we can get lined up. It will free me up to really focus on the party."

We say our good-nights, and I turn my body away from him, towards the moon glinting through the window. It's all for the best, I tell myself. It makes the most sense. The needs of the children should come first, and like he says, it has never been my forte.

There is no love that I have ever felt like the love I have for my children. But the chaos, uncertainty and complete messiness of being a mother has always grated at me. In the beginning it drove me to push harder, sleep less, work tirelessly to make sure everything was always in order. It forced me to seek greater perfection in my home, my appearance, my work, and my relationships. It seemed to be working.

But I can feel it caving in around me, like a weight upon my heart. I'm getting tired, slipping. I can't do it anymore, I surprise myself by thinking. There is a bitter pleasantness in that feeling of release. I drift into a fitful sleep.

I carefully complete my morning routine, seeing the girls off to school and making sure the twins are safely in the hands of the nanny. I cradle my cup of coffee as I enter my home office suite and settle in behind my desk. The ornate wall-length mirror opposite the desk reflects my immaculate appearance, but I look away from the dullness in my eyes. I'll definitely have to find another piece to accent that wall.

I throw myself into my work, prioritizing calling the staffing agency. Luckily, they have a great au pair candidate who is ready to begin immediately. I shift my focus to the upcoming birthday party, feeling slightly frantic that it is just a few days away. I go through each detail meticulously, ensuring that everything is finalized.

As I work, my mind weaves images, viewing outcomes that I then bring to life. I can see the bustle of the party, the sun flashing through our shade trees, children playing, and glasses clinking. Miranda and Samantha in their pristine summer dresses, and the twins looking dapper in matching suits and bow ties. I see myself on the arm of my husband, stunning and slender, jewelry flashing as I turn my head with a smile. And there is my Michael, handsome and tall, a look of bemused wonderment on his face as he looks down at me. The images start to fade as I recall his words from last night and the familiar anxiety encircles my heart.

My hands fly up to my mouth as I consider Michael's haunting behavior over the last few weeks and months. I tally up the hints and suspicions that triggered this extravagant party in the first place—a final hopeless effort to create the perfect family that I was afraid I was losing. A flood of images enters my mind: Miranda's smirking face, Samantha making her own dinner in the kitchen, Marcus and Julius, playfully relaxed as they joke with their nanny. Michael. Michael laughing into his phone, the coolness of the empty space between us at night, the disillusioned look in his eye as he spots my cocktail glass. His eyes that used to capture me and hold me up, a source of strength and deep love—eyes that now look through me.

My mind is reeling. Before I realize what I'm doing, I begin to devour articles online about infidelity and what can be done to win his attentions back. I have no concrete proof of course, I am simply curious, just satisfying a bit of curiosity. I find an article suggesting that I really cater to myself before even focusing on him. I struggle with that, feeling helplessly focused on what I can do to win him. The chilling thought follows that I don't really believe that he will come back to me. Feeling paralyzed by insecurity but determined to beat it back, I devise a plan to make myself better. I try to throw myself back into my work but find it impossible to focus. I decide that a strenuous hour or two at the gym might help to relieve the anxieties I am feeling.

Pulling up to the gym, I begin to remove my glasses. I hesitate, deciding to keep them on; using them as my mask for the day. I walk inside, absent-mindedly handing my key card over to the sign-in clerk. In a daze, I realize someone had been calling my name for some time. Snapping to, I turn and remove my shades. It is a man, a FINE man I have never seen before. Smiling, he beckons me over, taking my hand warmly. Laughing anxiously I pull back, apologizing for my spaciness. His eyes bore into mine, warm and curious. He introduces himself as James, the new fitness instructor. *Good God*, I wonder, *why is this man grinning at me so?*

"I'm making an effort to learn everyone's name here. I saw your profile, and right away I knew I wanted you to take my class." I look at him quizzically. "My technique is perfect for your goal profile, although from the looks of it, you are doing just fine."

Taken aback, my eyes widen, prompting another chuckle from him. "Still, it'd be nice to have you one day, for class?"

I laugh at his pleading tone. "Maybe." I smile, heading for the locker room. *Interesting,* I muse, grateful for a distraction from my own personal turmoil. I hit the treadmill hard, stretching out my legs as if to distance myself from the sadness inside me. I feel a sense of exhilaration as I push past my personal running record, running longer than I have in years. I can feel strength return to my body as I relish this sense of achievement, beginning to trust myself again. As I turn to head back to the locker room, I can see James watching me from across the room with his hands on his hips, smiling.

JEAN-MARIE

"MMMM...A GIRL COULD get used to this," I say luxuriously, an eclair in one hand and a glass of Cristal sparkling in the other. I roll my head back dramatically, moaning a little, and Simone and I burst out laughing.

We are relaxing at a table, shielded from the evening sun by an enormous white tent. Shouts of laughter echo up from the lawn, and the hum of adult voices merges with playful music. Colorful lanterns grace the ceiling, spilling over a banner that announces, "Happy Birthday Marcus and Julius!"

A server appears at the table and smiles in amusement as he clears away the clutter my children left behind. Marie and Jason barely touched the succulent fare before running off to join the festivities. Stephen has also made himself scarce, though his tactic is always to avoid the crowds. He has probably found a quiet place to read somewhere.

"Vanessa sure done it this time," I go on, shaking my head slowly as I gaze down the lawn at the small carnival taking place below. "My Jason will never be happy with a laser tag pizza party after this. I'm gonna be in trouuuble."

"Time to find yourself some new friends," Simone quips back with a smile. "Maybe someone who has a little class, instead of all this slumming." She giggles and I wink back at her. It's nice to see her let loose a little. This is the first time I've seen Simone since she broke down and ran off during our lunch date. We never did talk about it, and there are times tonight that I look at her and it seems to be hanging in the air between us. But I also haven't seen the playful side of Simone come out in weeks. Of course, it could have something to do with the cocktail in her hand. I've never known her to be much of a drinker.

"Ladiesss!"

We turn our attention to the back of the tent, where Ava is making her entrance. She strides over to our table, giving each of us a quick hug before setting her handbag down.

"Well, what have we here?" Ava chuckles as she surveys the celebration, her hands on her hips. She clucks her tongue. "Princess Nessa at her finest. And to think there are people starving in Africa. Just look at her out there!"

Turning my head, I set my eyes on the entire Wescott family, posing elegantly for a photographer as the party plays out in the background. Their attire is tastefully chosen to coordinate just enough, but not too much. I watch Vanessa fussing with Miranda's hair and then reassuming her stately posture. After a few flashes from the camera, Marcus screams and breaks away toward the merry-go-round, his nanny chasing him down.

Back at our table, we turn to each other and cascade into laughter. Though we don't understand Vanessa's need to throw such a lavish event, we're glad for the excuse to escape from our concerns and just be girls. We're making the most of it!

"So Ava," I say during a lull in our conversation, leaning

in close to her and choosing my words carefully, "what's been happening with your campaign? Every so often I see an article about it. Looks like things are getting a little...ugly."

She turns to me with an imperious look in her eye. "Oh, it's just the usual DC-politicking. I didn't expect any different. I mean, take a look at us," she gestures toward me and Simone with her brandy glass. "We black girls have risen up out of nothing. We came from nowhere, we found a hole in the system and beat it. It makes them uncomfortable...of course they couldn't leave my past alone." Her words are a strange mix of unshakeable confidence with an undercurrent of dark bitterness.

"It's so odd to me how quickly the news coverage shifted from being about the issues of running the most powerful city in this country," Simone ventures, "to delving into personal lives."

A loud laugh escapes Ava's lips. "Personal lives? It don't look to me like my rival Mr. Brad Thompson has had a personal life at all. Least nothing we've been able to pick up on. Perfect parentage, the right schools, the right circles. No ma'am, he's lilly white and squeaky clean. Mmm hmmm. It doesn't look like he's so much as stolen a hotel bath robe in the last fifty years." We all snicker at that, and the conversation moves to a safer subject.

Soon we hear Michael's voice over the sound system announcing that it's time to serenade the birthday boys and cut the cake. I link arms with Ava and Simone and saunter over to a small stage set up on the lawn that showcases a luscious tiered cake. Michael stands there grinning with his two boys, microphone in hand.

"Before we sing to Marcus and Julius, I would be remiss if I didn't acknowledge my beautiful wife, Mrs. Vanessa

Wescott." I spy Vanessa just to the side of the stage, looking radiantly up at her husband. "She has poured her vision and determination into every detail of this evening. After all, it's not every day that your three-year-olds, well, turn three! Let's all hope I can afford to pay for their weddings!"

The audience titters at his jest as I watch Vanessa's smile flicker. She quickly composes herself and joins her husband as the group erupts in a rendition of "Happy Birthday" and the boys blow out their candles.

The party winds down after that. The kids are returning from the festivities and we ladies head back to our table to start gathering our things. Vanessa breaks away from the crowd to say a quick good-bye before we leave for the night. Up close, her immaculate appearance is undermined by a weary look in her eyes. I give her a long hug.

"Honey, that was a beautiful night," I say, looking her in the eye. "You really outdone yourself. Are you feeling alright? Relieved that it's almost over?"

"Oh, yesss," she replies with a sigh, "I can't wait to get out of these shoes. Everything went off without a hitch. I can't believe I wasn't putting out more fires. My babies will never forget it," she smiles with satisfaction.

"You have the most gorgeous family," Simone exclaims. "You must be so proud. And that Michael of yours, the pair of you together is just perfect."

Ava interjects with, "What she really means to say is, 'Your man is FIIINE.'" We all snicker at that one.

Vanessa's expression suddenly looks a little fragile. "Yes, well, Michael's just about everything I ever wanted. But I wouldn't want to make you ladies jealous with the intimate details!" She looks relieved at our laughter and winks at us knowingly. I meet her eyes before she makes her exit. My gaze holds her quietly, curiously. She tosses up her head dramatically and walks away to say goodbye to her other guests.

I walk back to the car, hand-in-hand with Stephen, as the kids run on ahead. The summer moon is clear and serene. I reflect on my time with my girlfriends tonight, the drama and the laughter. *We sure do know how to have good time together*, I muse.

But I can't shake an unsettled feeling, something heavy pressing on me. I can't put my finger on it. I step into the car and relax into my seat while Stephen drives us home. As I continue to track the luminous moon, I have the elusive impression that my friends and I are, every one of us, broken.

There is something lurking just beneath the surface, something awful and unnamed. For all of the time we spend together, the texting and the phone calls and the laughter, we never seem to grow any closer. How can the sense of connection be missing?

What more are we searching for? Our words are hollow, our voices mere echoes of what they could be. I can see it in the eyes of every one of us—in Simone's silence, Ava's flippant laughter, Nessa's perfection. Finally my mind latches onto a thought that resonates within me. It fills me with sadness to comprehend that the void keeping us separate is a mutual feeling of shame. We are so fearful of rejection, so scared that if we are seen as we truly are, weaknesses and all, others will judge us as unworthy. We shut ourselves off, as if limiting our relationships will somehow make them stronger.

I shake my head and glare out into the night, resolving to change, desiring to live a life that's real.

AVA

I INSERT MY KEY into the door and step inside the dark flat, throwing my handbag and mail on the entry table and kicking off my heels. I revel for a moment in the stillness of this space. The boys are with Marlin this weekend and Clay is out of town at some training for top law enforcement, so I don't have to deal with any of my boys. I'm looking forward to a night by myself followed by a Sunday to get things done.

I slip out of my evening clothes and into a silky nightie, my mind still dwelling on Nessa's party as I go through my nightly routine in front of the mirror. I've known that girl since she was a vivacious sophomore at Spelman.

The day I met her I had just pulled up to the dorm to begin my final year as a Women's Studies major, purposefully arriving early so I could claim my room first. I went through check-in and when I found my room the door was already open and movers were hauling in upscale furniture and boxes. I entered the dorm with my shabby suitcase and threw a box onto the floor. There was Vanessa, perfectly accessorized, clasping a clipboard with French manicured fingernails.

I placed my hands on my hips and declared, "What the hell is going on up in here? Is this a dorm room or the Ritz Carlton?"

She looked me up and down, taking in my torn jeans and simple black tank, and raised an eyebrow.

"If I'm going to spend a whole year in this hole, I'm going to make it comfortable. Now I'll let you choose the bedroom you want, and you let me handle the common area. And the bathroom, cause we both know that's gonna to need some work. Now is this gonna work?"

So I got the room with the view and the classiest common space I had ever been into. It was strange sharing a dorm with Vanessa. She came from a life of wealth and privilege, I was the result of a one-night stand, second daughter of my single mama, so nothing was ever handed to me. Though I didn't show it, it took me a few weeks just to be comfortable going back to my dorm at night. What began as an uneasy alliance with Nessa soon developed into friendship. I was instrumental in humbling her prissy elitist ass, helping her let loose and see aaalllll of what Atlanta had to offer, and she likes to think that she brought a little of her style into my world of politics and power.

Now there she is, set up in a fancy white neighborhood with her model family and perfect life, giving parties like some society queen. I can't say I'm surprised at her life, only that most people's lives have a few more twists and turns; hers has always just fallen into place for her. Sometimes I don't think she's even real.

Things for me have more or less turned out the way I thought they would. After graduating from Spelman I left Atlanta for DC and never looked back. I stared as a staffer for a United States Senator from Georgia. I was drawn to the prestige of this city and spent a few years learning the ins and outs of the political elite. I moved up to become the Head of Staff, then became the Director of the Senate Appropriations Committee. I am relentless in pursuing my goals, so nothing was off the table…and I may or may not have used some of my sexual prowess to get where I wanted to go. As an ambitious, intelligent black girl but with no money to speak of, it was my biggest asset.

Men came in and out of my life, and how I finally settled down with Marlin I'll never know. I suppose it's because he was one for the few men I had ever met who refused to be manipulated or put up with my shit. Maybe I thought he might be good for me. He was in medical school at the time, and for a while I thought life could have some kind of fairy tale ending for me. We married and I got pregnant right away with Timothy. And I will be the first one to tell you that I have never been good at being a mama. I have no patience with that, and I don't care to. I know my boundaries and I'm not about to waste my time in things I'm no good at—someone else can handle that. Marlin was better at it than me. Even so, Timothy was in daycare as soon as they would take him so I could get back to work. Things at home went sour after that. I didn't have room in my world for the needs of a baby. My second son Andrew came along four years later, despite all of our attempts at contraception. The month after I had him, I went in for a complete elective hysterectomy, so that's the end of that.

Marlin and I tried to make our marriage work off and on. I had learned through years of practice to drop the things that weren't working for me, so my heart was never in it. Neither of us were faithful, or very happy, so a few years ago we finally ended it. The divorce could have been messier if we had wanted the same things. Marlin was granted custody of the boys as he wanted, and I got as much as I could financially which is what I wanted. I know it's not very motherly and sounds crass for me to say it, but nobody's ever accused me of being motherly.

I grab my computer and settle in on the chaise to get some strategizing done. My phone gives a short tone, a text message from Clay.

> *Long day, my presentation went well. Miss you tonight.*
> *See you.*

I smile smugly. I know I can catch me some men, they seem drawn to things they can't have. But it sure is nice to reel in one of them big fishes. I text back.

> *Girl time was fun tonight. Gotta get back to work. Later.*

Things with Clay are tight right now. He seems to get me—he knows when to push and when to back off. We're both so wrapped up in our work, that definitely takes priority, but we're fine with that. I'll admit, it's been some time since I've been with a man who was up to snuff. I've always had a certain power, especially when it comes to men. I don't even have to try. They are drawn to me somehow, and when they realize who they're dealing with, they seem to either cower—and I have no use for those pansies—or they try to assert their dominance, which leads to a pissing contest. And I don't have to tell you who usually comes out on top. But Clay is different. Oh, we have our brawls, but there is enough of a balance that we both feel in control, and it just works.

I turn back to my emails and send out a few replies, muttering to myself. I knew the campaign would be a tough one—this isn't my first rodeo. I've seen in all before. In the beginning everyone tries to make nice and shake hands and smile, but as the election draws nearer mud starts getting thrown and nothing is off the table. But I didn't understand the toll it would take. That night at the party to announce my campaign, I had felt so powerful, so self-assured, so certain. Almost as if God himself was giving me the green light. Since then I feel like I've been climbing up a brick wall, and my bare hands are busted and bleeding. I've had to pull out all the stops to assert myself, and everything is against me—my age, my color, my family, my past, even my damned vagina. I won't let it beat me. I'm a girl who gets what she wants. But I've never been so tired.

I snap my laptop shut and turn off the lights. For a while I sit up in bed, listening to the sounds of the city with my eyes closed. My body is tight and my mind is agitated. I find myself using a relaxing technique that Jean-Marie taught me years ago, and feel the tension in my shoulders ease away. "Holistic bullshit," I snigger to myself as I lay my head onto the pillow and drift away.

I am taken almost instantly to a memory filed deep away. The light is yellow and the air smells like childhood and cigarette smoke. I trace the pattern of the peeling wallpaper in the kitchen with my chubby finger until my motion is stopped by the bars of the play yard. I raise my head and feel the familiar sensation of hunger deep in my belly. The blanket moist beneath me. I am alone in the kitchen. I start to whimper and soon a little face appears through the bars. I feel my mouth turn up in a smile. My Gladys makes faces at me, crossing her eyes and wiggling her tongue. I laugh a little and reach out to feel the kinks in her hair. Soon I remember my hunger and begin to wail softly. She shushes me, brings me a drink, and climbs up the counter for a box of cereal. Her big toe shows through a hole in her sock. We play together quietly, my hunger easing as she feeds me through the bars of the crib.

I start awake to an urgent noise and it takes me several seconds to clear my head of the memory and return to the present. My phone is glowing with a call from an unrecognized number. The time is 3:47. I push the talk button and mumble something into the receiver.

"Mrs. Whitman?" The voice is male.

"Yea?"

"This is Sergeant Billman with the Metro Police. We've got your son Timothy here, and we need you to come down and pick him up."

I jolt upright as the cold press of fear washes over me. "Is he alright?" I ask frantically. My heart is pounding so loudly in my ears that my own voice sounds far away.

"He is uninjured." A pause. "We're holding him at the station on D Street Southeast, do you know how to get here?"

"D Street, I can find it."

I find my feet and tear into the bathroom, switching the light on before emptying the contents of my stomach into the sink. Uninjured. I straighten mechanically and stare into the mirror at my pallid face. I wash and pull my hair back. Breathe. I brush my teeth and head to the closet, stopping in the doorway with my hands pressed against the frame for support.

Remember your power, my mind is screaming at me. I want to throw on a robe and tennies and fly to my boy, but instead I choose a pair of tight jeans, a sleeveless shirt and some flats.

The streetlights flash past as I make my way through the city. The lightheadedness is gone, and in its place are images from news stories that have haunted me: a colored boy in a hoodie splattered with blood, flowers and a teddy bear on the sidewalk, a distraught mother sobbing into her hands. The cold fear grips my heart. I slam on the brakes, swerve into an empty spot and throw the car into park. I flip down the vanity mirror and stare into my own wild eyes.

"Ava Whitman, now you stop this right now." I stare myself down venomously. "You do not break down. You do not give in. You grab ahold of your power, and use it to get yours." I feel my resolve harden and the ice in my chest begins to fade.

I pause for a moment inside the front door. The station is busy. I see a blur of faces, black and white, uniformed and casual, but all tired and hard. Holsters and badges and handcuffs. For a moment I feel my body begin to shrink within itself, and then I snap my chin up higher.

"Excuse me," I call out to nobody in particular, with just a touch of attitude. "I'm here to pick up my son."

A stocky officer comes my way with a look of interest in his eye. I maneuver through my story and the paperwork carefully, keeping his attention but not playing my hand. I have not yet been recognized as Ava Whitman, mayoral candidate, who may soon be controlling every job in this place, and I want to keep it that way. The fact is, I'm scared out of my mind. I swallow up the fear and straighten.

"What can you tell me about Timothy's alleged crime?" I demand with a touch of superiority.

"Nothing really. But we have judges here working twenty-four hours," he offers with a shrug. "You'll know soon enough. I'll go and collect your son, and then you can proceed to the arraignment and get some answers."

I watch the officer's retreating figure and shake my head distastefully. Uninjured. I feel immense gratitude for that, and remind myself things could be so much worse. I wonder what he could have done. Timothy isn't the rebellious sort. He chooses the easiest path, something his father indulges but I could never abide. Not after fighting tooth and nail for every inch that I got. For Timothy, the easiest path means he barely made the grades to graduate high school and is now working a cash register and spending his nights with some hussy or other. No plans for college or the future. I guess I shouldn't be surprised.

I dwell bitterly for a moment on the fact that I am sitting here in a jail cleaning up this mess, instead of Marlin. He must be working a night shift at the hospital tonight. Then again, Timothy wouldn't be the first black teenager to be held without cause.

It is a jolt to my system to see him walked towards me by the officer, with this hands cuffed behind his back and his eyes downcast. He is wearing jeans with a T-shirt and jacket, and his pants hang a little awkwardly. They must have confiscated his belt. His eyes raise to meet mine, and I see an urgent panic in them as he assesses my face. I hold his gaze for a moment, taking in his distress. He looks defeated.

"You okay?" I ask, placing a hand on his arm firmly.

"I think so," he answers softly.

"Then hold up your head," I command with authority. "We're going in to see the judge, and he's not gonna want to hear any sniveling. I don't know what you've done, but you're going to stand up, man up, and face it. You can do this," I say with a softer tone. "Now let's go."

The officer nods his head and walks us through several hallways to a small courtroom area. There are a few cases in front of ours, a drunk and someone accused of assault.

The judge, an older white woman, looks exhausted and keeps glancing at the clock.

Eventually an officer calls out, "Whitman, Timothy," and I watch my son walk to a podium stationed in front of the judge. She gazes down at him wearily. I feel anger course through my body at the dull look in her eye.

"This Timothy Whitman is accused of attempted grand theft of an automobile and evading arrest. How do you plead?"

Timothy looks up. I can see the vein in his neck pulsing, the effort it is costing him to stand up so straight.

"You mean, 'guilty or not guilty?'" he asks loudly, though I can hear the tremor in his voice.

"Yes," the judge answers, and her voice has softened slightly.

"Not guilty."

"Court date will be set for September twenty-third," the officer continues efficiently. "After an assessment of the accused's condition, as a life-long resident of the DC area and considering his parentage, he is not considered a flight risk and no bail is recommended."

"Parentage?" the judge queries.

"Yes, Your Honor. His father is a nurse practitioner at Sibley Memorial. Mother," the officer sneaks a look in my direction, "is Ava Whitman, current candidate for Mayor of DC."

I hold my head up defiantly as all eyes in the room turn to me. Well, there's the end of that secret. After the dirt that my opposition has dug up on me already—my childhood, divorce and sexual intrigues—I know this little incident will be online and blown out of proportion within hours. I return the judge's gaze steadily, and then chance a hint of a smirk. I will not let them get me.

Hours later, when Timothy has been delivered to his father and the yelling is over, I find myself back in the sanctuary of my apartment. I turn off my cell and close every curtain, shutting out the light of day. I open a bottle of Jack, drain every drop, and curl up under my duvet without undressing. "Go hard or go home," I slur aloud as I drift into nothingness.

SIMONE

"GOOD MORNING, BABY," I smile at the bleary-eyed boy emerging from the bedroom. You mean "man," I correct myself as I watch Daniel mumble and reach for a mug to share in my coffee. "How was your night?"

He raises his index finger at me to wait a moment while he takes a long gulp. "It was good, Mom. Went to see a movie with some friends, then got some grub after. It's going to kill me today though. I'm tired."

Daniel has been working days for a lawn maintenance company to build up some savings. Covering his college tuition shouldn't be a problem, what his scholarships aren't bringing in I can provide. But he's always been a hard worker and wants to be able to pay for his own expenses outside of rent. It makes me proud.

"Want to go out to dinner tonight?" I suggest. I notice an eyelash has fallen down on his cheek, and reach over to wipe it away, but he pulls back, dodging my touch.

"Mom, please," he says with a hint of frustration.

"What? I'm just getting an eyelash," I reply defensively.

"I got it, Mom." His hand passes over his face a few times. "Look mom, I know I'm going away in a few weeks. I know it's not an easy time for you, but I really need you to ease off."

"It's just an eyelash," I laugh dismissively. "Lighten up."

"No, Mom!" He pounds his mug down on the counter. "Listen to me. It's not about an eyelash. Things are changing for me. Big things. Jobs and girls and college. But when I walk through this door, everything is the same. You want me to be your little guy, doing dinner and having movie nights and getting my eyelashes. Well, I can get my own damn eyelash!" His fiery eyes meet mine. "When are you going to start treating me like an adult?"

Whoa, I think to myself as I watch his outburst. Where is this coming from? I know things have been a little strained, and maybe I've been a little…needy? From what's going on at work? I look up at my son with troubled eyes.

"I'm sorry, baby," I say, and immediately regret my choice of epithet. He rolls his eyes at me and mumbles something about having to get to work before trudging out of the kitchen. The eyelash is still stuck to his cheek.

I put my fingers to my forehead and lean on the counter with my elbows. What I mess I just made of that.

I look back over our relationship during the past few weeks, and there is something to his accusation. It's just that Daniel has been the core of my life for so long, and he seemed to be the only thing I was doing well at. My one success, raising an amazing son, while my business falls apart and my love life idles. I can see where I've been using him as an escape from my realities, and I despise myself for it.

The thud of the bathroom door closing interrupts my reverie and I glance at the clock. I need to get moving or I'll be late for this morning's briefing with the forensic consultants.

Gathering my purse and slipping into my heels, I consider knocking on the bathroom door and saying my good-bye to Daniel, but I think better of it and walk out the front door, locking it softly behind me.

The metro is busier than usual today, and I arrive at the office with just minutes to spare. I hate being late—I feel like it puts me at a disadvantage. I have always prided myself in being prepared and put together. I make my way straight to the conference room, where the others are already waiting.

"So sorry I'm late," I say, taking my seat. "The metro was insane today."

"No trouble, we've just arrived ourselves," Maxwell responds with a casual smile.

The problem with working with Maxwell is that I can't look at him without noticing his eyes. They are as hypnotic as the day I first met him, a rich hazel in the middle and then flaring out to a clear green that contrasts with his dark complexion. My attraction to him keeps me constantly on my guard, but I've been able to keep things professional between us.

The briefing lasts nearly three hours. The consultants mapped out a strategy to try to thoroughly examine our internal records and bank records, and so far everything is aligning—no red flags to indicate any errors or fraud. A feeling of hopelessness enters my chest and presses on me as we continue our discussion, but I am able to keep a level head. The consultants have some other theories that they are going to pursue, including a review of our client accounts and even our employees to see if anything comes up. But I can tell by their analysis that things aren't looking good.

"Henry," I turn to the controller, "what kind of a time-frame are we talking about here? How long can we keep things running as they are, before we run out of funds to back these payroll runs?"

Henry clears his throat, looks down at his computer and makes some quick adjustments. "We should be good for the run this coming Friday, but we might not be able to meet the one three weeks from now."

I can feel the color drain from my face. I close my eyes for a moment, my head reeling with a rush of thoughts. Three weeks. I had put so much trust in the consultants' ability to find what we had been missing, I could think of no contingency plan. I kept my company lean. I could not lose any of my employees and keep the doors open. My eyes fly open.

"What are the legal ramifications," I say, "of my making a personal loan to the business to keep us going longer?" I turn to Maxwell. "How much time do I need to buy you to finish up your forensic examination?"

"I should be able to complete things by the end of next week at most." Maxwell responds, then leans in closer, his face intent. "As far as the money goes…Technically, making a loan to Ingenuity will not affect your protected personal status. However, I do need to warn you that the more the lines are blurred between your personal finances and the finances of this company, the more you may be liable if you do come under legal investigation. For this purpose, I would not recommend it. Not until we can get to the bottom of what is happening with your funds."

I consider his words carefully, and before long our discussion has come to an unsettling close. I watch Henry exit the room with the others, the anxiety subtly apparent in his face. I wonder if he has a back-up plan for if things go bad. I hate that circumstances are forcing me to suspiciously examine my employees, searching for one who has both the authority and the motive to bring us down. I've always tried to look for the best in people—it goes against my grain. I exhale slowly.

I look up to see Maxwell's tall form in the doorway. "May I have a moment, Simone?" he asks, closing the door behind him and talking a seat.

"Of course," I respond. "What's on your mind?"

"I know it's not my place, but I really feel strongly about this," he says, looking straight at me. "I've seen a lot of businesses going through this type of thing. Some make it through, and some collapse. It's not a pretty thing to see, but it happens. And the worst part about it is when the owner gets annihilated with it. I've seen people lose their savings, their homes, their reputations. I don't want to see that happen to you," he says softly. "I can tell that this company means a lot to you, and that you put a lot into it. But in the end, it's only a business. Don't give up your life for it."

I look down at my hands pensively as he walks back to the door. "I just couldn't leave without saying it."

By the time I glance back up, he has gone. I sit in silence for a long time, considering my options. Finally I shake my head and reach for my cell phone. I can't just do nothing. I can't ignore my employees. I can't ignore my clients. There are simply too many lives at stake here for me to place so much value on mine.

"Hello? This is Simone Orchard. I need someone to help me transfer some funds."

❧

It's been a few days since the blow-up with Daniel. Things at home are a little icy. He has been going out with his friends more and coming in later. I'll get a cryptic text once in a while, but that's about it. I'm trying not to stress too much about it, not blow it out of proportion. I am giving him as much space as possible, but I get the impression that he may need me now more than ever. Then I think back to my last couple years of high school and the strained relationship with my parents. I know it isn't unusual for kids to pull away at this point. It gives me some courage to trust Danny, and allow him to come to me when he's ready. Today he left with his landscaping team to do an extended project at a nearby resort and he won't be home for a few days. I hope it will give him the time he needs to cool off.

My loan to Ingenuity has gone through. I know Henry was relieved at the extra time that it gives us, but I caught Maxwell with a troubled look on his face after I told him. We are all working longer hours, trying to get as much done as possible, knowing how limited our time is.

I'm reviewing personnel files after hours tonight, searching through the profiles of our executive and finance teams to see if there is anything amiss. I'm checking police records and social media too, trying to be as thorough as possible. It would be funny if the situation wasn't so serious—I just learned that decades ago my head of HR was an exotic dancer. Through my office glass I can see Maxwell, pouring over some files in the conference room. He has loosened his tie, his sleeves are rolled up, and when he turns his head I can see the furrow is apparent in his brow. I honestly don't know that much about him, other than he's divorced and taking pilot lessons on the weekends.

I decide that I deserve a little break, and giggle to myself as I search the name "Maxwell Ellis" in the public records search site. Nothing too incriminating here, some parking tickets and some old addresses. Looks like he is originally from upstate New York. I pull up his Facebook profile next, and for once allow myself to become fully absorbed by his eyes in the profile picture. I feel my body start to respond, heat rising up from my chest as I investigate this man working in the room across the hallway.

My cell phone vibrates suddenly, and I hastily close the browser. You'd think I'd been on a more erotic site than Facebook, I laugh at myself as I check the text message. It's from an acquaintance from my networking group, asking if I have seen the local news. I frown to myself, re-open my browser and pull up a news site. Looks like typical DC drama, poverty and some mud-slinging over the upcoming mayoral race. I truly don't know how Ava does it. My phone vibrates again—another text from the parent of one of Daniel's lacrosse buddies, asking if that was my business on the news. My heart starts to beat faster as I furiously scan the headlines scrolling across the bottom of the web site. Finding nothing there, I enter the words "Ingenuity Payroll" in the search field.

A story pops up in the feed with today's date, published one hour ago. "Local Payroll Company in Financial Meltdown" the headline reads. "Paychecks and HSAs for thousands in the DC workforce at risk."

With shaking hands I drill down into the article, and my breath catches in my throat as the screen flashes with a picture of myself. As I frantically scan the article, words like "mismanagement of funds," "executive extravagance," "backs of the working poor," and "whistleblower" enter my mind like physical blows. My phone is vibrating desperately now, and my computer starts to ping repeatedly as a flow of incoming emails from employees and clients barrages my account.

I rise from my desk and lean back into the wall in shock. "Maxwell," I hear myself calling out as I continue to stare dully at the computer screen. He appears quickly at my side, prompted by some desperation in my voice, and leans in to read through the article.

"Holy shit," he says vehemently, sitting down in my seat. "Where did this come from? It's certainly premature. They have no evidence to back this story! None of this is substantiated, they are only citing a source within the company. Media sensationalism, publishing before they get the story straight. Holy shit."

A heavy silence permeates the room as I wrestle with my thoughts. One of my employees leaked this out? My head is swimming and my knees feel weak. I thought I had more time. I thought we were going to work this out internally, that it would never get this far. As if from far away, I can hear my phone buzzing and an erratic ping from the incoming emails. My resolve hardens and I snap to awareness, instantly feeling Maxwell's eyes on me.

"Okay," I say, kicking off my heels and striding back to my seat. Maxwell is rising slowly, stepping back and allowing me to reclaim my space. "Would you find Jonathan and see if he can come in tonight? We sure could use a lawyer around here."

"Yeah," he replies gently, but his eyes continue to search mine. "Simone, are you okay?" As he speaks the words, one of his hands reaches towards me, into the empty space between us. "Is there anything I can do?"

I look down at his hand, perceiving the invitation it contains. I raise my head back up to his eyes, and see in them my weakness, my feminine frailty, my insecurities, my need. With a faint shake of my head, I respond authoritatively, "I'm okay, Max. Thanks."

He turns to leave and I watch his retreating frame with mixed emotions. I sit down and start sorting through my emails, trying to come up with some good responses for maximum damage control. A few minutes later I am startled by the thought that I had called him Max.

☙

I wake with a start in the morning, my mind sluggishly putting together the pieces of the previous night. As the picture becomes clearer, the press of a weight upon my chest increases and I find myself fighting for breath.

I need help, I think to myself. I need to talk to someone. I reach for my phone and switch it on. I had finally turned it off completely last night in an attempt to silence my mind. I go to my contacts and search through the names urgently. Only after some time do I realize that I am looking for my mom. I freeze as the memories wash back over me relentlessly –California, the accident, the loneliness, the pain. I know I need to cry and release some of these emotions, but I am wrung out by the intensity of the last few hours and can only lie there limply. I glance at the clock. It is still early, but I have to be ready and present today to mitigate damage and be there for my employees. But I know I need to talk to someone. I send out a text to Jean-Marie, praying she is the safe harbor I'm looking for.

I put on one of my favorite dresses that I refer to as my "smart dress" because of its linear and clean look and I pin my hair up. I walk past Daniel's room, wishing I could hold him and at the same time glad that he is working at the remote site. I don't want him to have to see me like this.

My day proceeds around me with sharp clarity, though I have the distinct sensation that I'm watching my life happen instead of living it. I call an emergency meeting of all Ingenuity staff, explaining our situation and taking questions. As I do my best to be transparent and quell their fears, the knowledge that one of them has betrayed me is ever-present in my mind. With the help of my attorney, I send out a press release to local media outlets but decline any requests for interviews. I'm just not ready for that yet. I spend hours with the marketing team, reaching out to clients and trying to persuade them to stick with us.

At the end of the day, I gather my things and turn out the light in my office. It's after hours, but some of my key team members are staying late. Jean-Marie and I were able to connect through text, and she offered to pick me up for dinner. I only feel a little guilty about slipping away. I know I need to confide in a friend in order to keep going. I wave good-bye to Maxwell, who is reading through some personnel files with a pensive look on his face.

I watch Jean's car arrive from the lobby window and meet her at the curb.

"Hey there, girl! What's happening?" Jean-Marie starts in, and then her tone changes. "Honey, you alright?" her forehead pinches with concern as she watches me buckle in. "You look a sight."

I stare ahead for a long while, unsure. It's clear that Jean hasn't seen my news. She is definitely the most genuine, selfless friend that I have out here. She's never let me down. I want to tell her everything, but I realize that I have been building a wall around the most vulnerable parts of myself. I feel tears well up and slip silently down my cheeks, and the embarrassment is swallowed up in gratitude for the feeling of release.

"Hhmmm," Jean-Marie muses, driving away from the office. "Something tells me this isn't a restaurant kind of night. We need takeout. Let's go to your place—I guarantee it'll be quieter—and eat our feelings. Followed by a trip to the liquor store," she glances at me and laughs. "Maybe we need to hit that liquor store first."

I feel a space begin to open up in my chest, and the bitter tears that fall are laced with relief.

At my apartment, over chow mein and a bottle of Chateau Ste. Michelle, I open up to Jean about the battles I am facing at work. I am tentative at first, feeling a sense of guilt over my own innocence and lack of experience, feeling somehow culpable for the turn of events, as if I could have avoided them if I were just sharper, smarter, more capable.

"Simone, I'm glad you're sharing this with me. You can talk to me about anything. We've all had setbacks. Lord knows I have."

I sense the sincerity of Jean's words, her openness with me and empathy for my situation, the words become easier to say. We cry together and laugh together, and I begin to feel an underlying sense of peace despite the uncertainties of my future.

AVA

I AM STANDING IN Marlin's kitchen with my hands on my hips, my expression fierce. Marlin is leaning against the bar nursing a beer and Timothy sits at the table, looking down at his hands. It has been a week since Timmy's arrest, and I have been so busy at campaign events and putting out the media fires that keep springing up that this is the first time we've been able to get together and hash this out.

"You have no idea how this is impacting my campaign!" I rage in the silence. "As if I didn't have enough to deal with, with all those establishment sons of bitches trying to keep the black girl out of their club. Now here it is, splashed all over the media, a confirmation of all their suspicions and stereotypes. There she is, mayoral candidate Ava Whitman, escorting her teenage son from the jailhouse. Ain't that pretty?! The woman who aims to direct the local police has raised a son who spends his weekends hot-wiring Jeep Cherokees in the street."

"Whoa, whoa, Ava, power down," Marlin takes a step towards me with exasperation, his hands raised defensively. "This is not all about you. I won't have you putting this all on Timmy like that. You haven't even heard him out. And you know that most of the dirt surrounding your campaign is dirt you dug yourself."

My eyes blaze and my fists are clenched. That bastard, so calm, so level-headed. There he goes again, turning our little men into pussies who don't have to earn a damn thing, and throwing me under the bus in the process. My breath is heavy, and before I realize it I am looking wildly around the room for something to throw. I stop myself and close my eyes tightly. There is a brief, dark sensation of vertigo, as if I am tumbling out of control. I consciously steady my breath, leaning back against a wall.

My eyes snap open and I stare out at the kitchen. Timothy and Marlin are watching me intently, as if I am some wild, uncontrollable thing that may strike. Timmy's eyes are hooded with fear. I hate what I see in them. I hate myself. I feel my anger dissolve into apathy, and I calmly approach the table and sit down across from my son.

"Fine," I say with a cool calmness. "I'm waiting to hear what happened, Timmy."

Timothy starts slowly, his gaze lifting up to his father for support.

"Okay. I was out late that night. I had been over to Derek's house, it was just the two of us playing video games. You can ask his mom. She was there the whole time," he directs at me.

"Were you drinking? Drugs?" I ask automatically.

"Just a couple beers mom, I swear," he replies. "Nothing hard and no, no drugs." I nod my head. So far, it rings true to me. And I can smell a lie a mile away.

"A little after midnight I decided to split, so I hopped on the metro to get back home. It was pretty dead out, I was the only one sitting in the car. At the next stop there was a big commotion outside, some yelling, and soon these two white guys came running into the car and quickly sat down apart from each other. They were trying to look really nonchalant, you know, like they were hiding something. Anyway, a little bit later a couple of cops came into the car."

Timothy pauses for a moment, and I can tell that he is trying hard to keep his emotions in check. I can feel the anger rising in me again, and get ready to pounce on him if he can't keep it together. He looks straight down at his hands, takes a breath and continues.

"They came in and started yelling, told us to put our hands in the air and get down on our knees. I know it's stupid," he continues, "I know I'm a black kid, that I should do whatever the cops tell me. But it didn't register at first that they were talking to me. I knew I hadn't done anything. So I stood up and tried to tell them what had just happened, you know, that the other guys had just come running in. So I stood up and started talking …," his voice trails away again.

"And the next thing I knew, one of the cops had his gun out, and he was aiming it right at my chest. I stopped and sort of stared in shock. He told me to put my hands in the air, and get down on my knees, and so I did." He stops and stares down for a long time.

"And it scared the living shit out of him," Marlin continues for him. "and they cuffed him, and yanked him along to the patrol car, and sat him down right in between the other two guys. When he tried to talk to them in the car, they told him to shut up. They booked him and threw him in a cell with a bunch of other adults because he is eighteen. Men who were drunk, men who were crazy," Marlin concludes. "And one of the officers had to call his you for him, because Iwas on shift and couldn't answer the phone, and he was too damn scared to call you himself."

I hold Marlin's gaze as that sinks in, pushing down the feeling of self-loathing and ignoring the implications. "Alright. I believe you. Wrong place, wrong damn time," I finish, shaking my head. "So what are we going to do now?"

"Court date is in a few weeks," Marlin says. "I've contacted a good attorney, we're going to meet with him next week. I know your schedule is packed, so I'm sure I can handle most of this myself. It should be a clean case. What I need from you," he continues, leaning towards me on the table, "is a little compassion. A little support. I've got a fishing trip set up next weekend for my birthday, and the boys will be with you. I need you to be there for them."

I stand up from the table and gather my purse. "I can live with that," I say. "You're sure it's a good attorney? I can get some recommendations. The last thing he needs is a permanent mark on his criminal record. Not to mention the fines or the jail time."

"I've got it covered," Marlin replies. "We just need to wait it out, stick together until it blows over."

"Ha! Easy for you to say. It's not your face being splashed all over the internet every day," I sneer as I head out the door. "I'll see you next weekend."

I shake my head as I stride back to my car. I step inside and close the door against the hum of the city around me. Turning over Timothy's story in my mind, I realize that I was so wrapped up in the confrontation with Marlin that I hadn't given my son a parting glance.

∽

Clay has reserved a table for us tonight at Plume, a swanky destination for the movers and shakers of DC. I've been so uptight all week that I decided to get a massage before our date to ease my nerves and clear my head. I'm feeling a bit more like myself as I step inside the grand foyer of The Jefferson Hotel on Clay's arm, wearing a sexy emerald evening dress and my favorite stilettos. I watch one of the bell boys notice me and smile, settling back into my power. I relish the feel of strutting across the polished marble next to this gorgeous man, the feeling of being unconquerable.

Our table is tucked away in a secluded corner, giving us plenty of privacy to talk about our world of intrigues. Clay takes his office of District Attorney very seriously and he never divulges more to me than is strictly legal—but my awareness of the gossip around DC allows me to fill in the blanks. We lean in together intimately in the dim light, our knees often touching. Clay is attentive and charismatic tonight, as usual, but I'm sensing that there is something on his mind.

"There is a new case that's come across my desk recently," Clay mentions smoothly, swishing his glass of Madeira. "I hesitate to mention it to you, but I think it's better that you have some foreknowledge. I know the campaign smut has been hitting you hard lately."

I roll my eyes a little bit, polishing off the bite on my fork. "Oh, that. Well, it sure as hell hasn't been the best week of my life, but it's going to take a lot more than a legal snafu with my teenage son to break me. Besides, he is completely innocent, you'll see during the trial that it was a clear case of being in the wrong place at the wrong time. Honestly, the judge would have thrown out the case if it hadn't been my boy standing there."

Clay looks straight into my eyes, as if to discern some hidden meaning underneath my words. "I'm sorry about your son," he goes on, shaking his head a little. "I hope they get to the bottom of it and exonerate him quickly. But that's not the case I was referring to."

"Oh?" I keep my words casual while searching his face for some clue.

"I know you're familiar with Simone Orchard but how familiar?" he continues, leaning forwards slightly.

I blink a couple of times and look over at him quizzically. "Oh, sure. She's a close friend—I mean she's a recent addition to my circle. You know, Vanessa Wescott and Jean-Marie, Simone. Not my favorite, if I'm being real. I'm surprised that she's lasted very long in DC business, much too polite to get much done in the real world. You've met her," I recall. "I introduced you at Timmy's award ceremony. What have you got on her?"

"She's had some business troubles recently," Clay goes on. "You've heard of Ingenuity Payroll? The local company that's going belly-up?"

"Wait, the business that's swallowed up all those HSA accounts?" I ask incredulously. "That's Simone's company? Holy damn." I lean back in my chair and shake my head. Simone Orchard, so gracious, all the time skimming other people's money.

"It's causing quite a bit of uproar, simply because if effects so many locals. Some in the office are lobbying to have all of her personal assets frozen. And there's more to it than that," he says, and I watch the creases appear on his forehead. "She made a donation to your campaign. Nothing sizeable, just a token, but I've become aware that the Thompson campaign caught wind of it. You can be sure they will milk it for all it's worth."

Clay's handsome face swims a little before me. I glance over at the glow of a nearby lantern and try to process this new development. One more thing, one step closer to what is beginning to feel like the ledge of a precipice instead of a finish line. Failure. The word echoes dissonantly in my heart, and I dig deep within myself and summon the fierce strength that I need.

"There's no way for you to put a lid on it?" I ask.

"Nothing I can do. It's out of my hands." His response is quick, almost disinterested.

"Oh, there's always something that can be done," I gaze over at him, willing my seductive prowess to take over. "I know you have all those contacts, know all the right people …"

"No, Ava. That isn't going to work with me."

"Fine." I look away. "I'll call a press conference next week to do some damage control if it gets leaked. I'll assert that I barely know her, simply a friend of a friend, which is the honest truth. Cite all of the other campaign donations I've received. It will pass, people forget." I glance over at Clay and catch a glint in his eye that unhinges something within me. I know what he is about to say before he says it.

"Ava," He straightens in his chair and something ripples along his square jaw. "You know how I feel about you. You're sexy, passionate, you keep me on my toes, and I love that in a woman. We have been good together these past few months. But I've got to start thinking about what being with you means for my career long-term. Your past, that's one thing. But the legal entanglements, the things that I see come across my desk…"

He pauses for a moment and I detect a wariness in his eye. "It's effecting my work, my rapport at the office. I can't afford that. I know this is a bad time to do it, but it's how I feel right now. I think we need to take a break."

I automatically sit up straighter, my head held high, and raise my eyebrow. "Oh, you think you can do better?"

I muse deliberately and take a sip of wine, an eerie coldness in my voice. "You think you can jump in and out of my bed anytime it suits you? Mr. District Attorney DiNofrio, finest lawyer in the land, dismissing his woman as soon as things get gritty. Some man you are, Clay. What a man. So supportive, so strong.

You haven't got balls enough to sit out two flimsy court cases. Well, to hell with you. You abandon me now, there is no going back." I set my wine glass back down on the table with cool indifference. Maintaining eye contact, I grab my clutch and stand up imperiously from the table. "So long, Mr. DiNofrio."

I can feel his gaze upon my back as my heels click sharply along the corridor. I break out into the sultry night, alone, and find myself gasping for air. Clay's words linger in my mind, and I feel for a moment as if I am drowning. I breathe deliberately into the night, and my resolve hardens around me. I am Ava Whitman, strong and ferocious, and I have never needed a man to get what I want. Clay, Timothy, Simone—they are simply hurdles for me to leave behind me in my race to get to the top. I stand up straighter and viciously silence the voices whispering in my mind.

In time I find my cell phone and call a cab. A text message from Jean-Marie pops up, and I realize I've been ignoring her all week. She's starting to get concerned about me, having heard the news about Timothy. I mull it over dully in my mind, and determine that I shouldn't text her. I can't see her, speak to her. Not Jean. Not right now. She's too close, too intuitive. If I were to let her in right now, it would break me. I don't realize that the taxi has pulled up until the driver taps his horn and pulling me out of my daydream.

VANESSA

THE MORNING SUN glints against the wrought-iron gate of the driveway, and I wish I had grabbed my sunglasses. I relish the feel of the cooler air against my skin, grateful the summer is coming to a close. I head back into the garage, find the step ladder and navigate up the rungs—not an easy task in heels. I find the box labeled "Fishing Stuff" and pull. The box jerks forward awkwardly, nearly emptying its contents, but I steady it at the last second and make my way down the ladder to safety.

"Baby, I found the fishing box," I announce to Michael as I set my load down in the mudroom.

"Thanks hon," he responds absent-mindedly, checking the time on his watch. He is in preparation mode, pacing around the house, packing and checking things off of his list. I've spent the morning working on the design layout for a client's new guest house and decided to take a break to help get Michael out the door. He's been surprisingly excited about this getaway—fishing isn't his typical diversion—and he certainly deserves it, what with all the time he has been spending at the hospital over the last few months. I have been focusing my energy on being fully supportive, though a shadowy thought lingers in my mind, the anxiety that he would rather be with the guys than with me.

"Almost ready," he mutters as his phone rings from inside his back pocket. He zips up his duffel, checks the number on the phone display and smiles. "Hey," he answers, his back to me. "Yep, I'm just getting into the car. I should be there in half an hour. See you soon."

My eyes rest on the line of his shoulder, the precision of his haircut. I feel an urge to step behind him and wrap my arms around his waist, but for some reason his body feels off-limits to me. It has been a long time—too long—since we have been intimate. I've brought it up twice before but it has just sparked a conversation about schedules and fatigue, followed by sex that felt awkward and hollow. Maybe it's his aging, his drive is slowing down. Maybe it's my aging, I'm just not that attractive anymore. I push the thought away.

"Time to go?" I say, and my own voice sounds too chipper and false. He turns to me with a half-smile.

"Yep! I can't wait to get out of the city and get some fresh air. Thanks for handling everything while I'm away, hon. I really appreciate it."

His voice is sincere as he approaches me and squeezes me into a quick hug. As he releases me, I look into his face and lean in for a kiss, which he administers perfunctorily.

"Take good care of the kids. And I don't know what kind of cell reception I'll have out there, so I might not be in touch until Sunday. Love you."

I watch him drive away, the heaviness churning inside me. Time passes as I stare out at the empty driveway. My trance is broken by the echoes of my giggling toddlers, playing with the nanny downstairs. I feel a sudden disconnect in my mind, like something has snapped, irreparable. I am going insane. I frown, grab a bottle at random from the kitchen, and head back to my home office to finish that guest house design.

⁂

Later that night, I am curled up on a chaise in the darkness of my living room, listening to the quiet of the house. Miranda is watching a movie in her room, and Samantha and the boys have been tucked in by the au pair, so the house is mine. I run my manicured fingernails over the expensive upholstery of the chaise and have a sudden, unbridled desire to claw through the material. I freeze, unsettled by the thought, and then laugh at myself instead. The sound is shrill in my ears. I need to talk to someone.

I play with my phone for a while and consider who I might call. Michael is out of the question—I'm sure he's getting sauced with the guys and is probably out of cell range, anyway. I hope he's getting sauced with the guys. That terrible tightness inside me clenches again, and I toy with the idea that he is cheating on me. Found someone younger, someone whose body doesn't bear the scars of three pregnancies. Maybe she's white and would fit in better in his world. Someone perfect who can keep their shit together and be what he deserves.

I drop the phone. As I gather it up, I remember that I was looking for a friend to call. There's Ava, of course, my oldest friend, but lately she's had so much going on, so busy with the campaign that we haven't been able to connect.

Simone might have been an option, but I haven't seen her since I got word that her business was folding and I don't want to get tangled up in that mess. I consider Jean-Marie, and realize that I don't want to talk to her. She sees through me, and God knows I don't need that right now. I need someone to laugh with. Ava it is.

As I hear her pick up, excitement surges through me. I didn't realize how much I needed to connect with someone.

"Simone, Simone," she sings out dramatically. "What you calling for this late on a Friday night? I know Michael's out of town and all, but if you're looking for a bootie call you got the wrooong number."

The laughter feels like coming home. "Well Madam Mayor Whitman, your schedule is so packed with power players that I knew the middle of the night was the only time you would deign to chat with little old me," I say, and add with a wicked smile, "That is, as long as I'm not interrupting anything important between you and a certain district attorney."

Her laughter peels out over the phone, a little discordant. "Nope, nope, I'm going stag tonight. I'm just here with my boys having a night in. Gotta step up and play mama while Marlin is out fishing with the guys. So for the boys it's action movies and pizza and I've been catching up on some work."

A part of me is relieved to hear her say it, confirming Michael's story of his weekend away. I silently berate myself for entertaining so many doubts.

"Michael was so excited to get away. Things at the surgery can be so stressful for him—I'm glad he was able to make it. A trip out with the guys was just what he needed." I feel the strange jealousy returning and focus on Ava's words.

"I guess you've heard about Timmy's arrest," she is saying. "Biggest mess of policing I've ever seen. He happens to be in the same metro car as two white crooks, and they haul him in, too. Treated him like trash at the station. I tell you, I can't wait to get in there as mayor and clean things up. Heads are gonna roll."

"I'm sorry about all that, hon. How is Timmy doing?"

"Oh, he's alright. He was shaken up, but he's going to get through it. It's good for him to have a taste of real life, maybe help him man up a bit and do something with himself. It sure is messing with my campaign, though. Every damn day there's been something about it in the papers. Brad Thompson sure knows how to conduct a smear campaign, I'll give him that. Have you heard about Simone?"

"Yeah, I saw her in the papers," I respond. "She looked like hell. I always knew she would have trouble in the District—too trusting, wide-eyed to make it here. Like she was always trying too hard. It was only a matter of time 'til she got stepped on."

"You think she did it?" Ava gossips back. "Sure would be a good cover, all sweet and friendly, all the while siphoning money from all those accounts. I know Jean-Marie wouldn't like to hear it, but I can believe it. Everybody has an angle, even simpering Simone." We laugh together and our bond seems to deepen over the ugliness of our words.

"That's not the end of it, either," Ave continues with a new spitefulness in her voice. "Simone made a donation to my campaign months ago, and the media might catch wind of it. One more puddle of mud they'll drag me through. You know, I might actually be able to win this campaign if the people around me would quit making dumb-asses of themselves."

"I made a donation too, you know," I respond, trying to lighten things up. "I'll try to stay out of the papers—or at least not get caught for any of my felonies until after November. You got this though, hon. You're the toughest woman I know. And at least you've got Clay by your side."

"Yeah, there's that," she says distractedly. "How about you? How is Princess Nessa fairing these days?"

"Oh, things here are just fine," I answer. "I'm finishing up some designs that will be featured in a national publication—I'll let you know which magazine picks it up. Kids are great," my voice falters a little, but I finish strong. "Things with Michael have never been better. I don't know what I'd do without him."

The connection goes silent for a moment. I regroup and give Ava an animated good-bye before hanging up. I try to hang on to the jovial tone that began our conversation, but I find only heaviness has taken its place. I climb up the stairs and escape into an isolated sleep.

❧

The burning in my calves intensifies and I change the angle of the treadmill and adjust my stride. I have been running for nearly an hour, and I can still feel the fire of adrenaline surging through my body. It is a foreign feeling for me, to be so agitated and out of control. I take a drink from the bottle of water in front of me and focus on my breathing.

From the moment I woke up this morning I have had an undeniable drive to fix—everything. Before I had even left the bedroom I was rearranging the furniture. I moved even the heavy pieces, surprised by my own strength, but soon decided that I want to purchase a new furniture package entirely. I left the disaster I had made upstairs to join my kids in the kitchen. The au pair was making waffles and Samantha and the boys were munching happily, syrup and strawberries dripping all over the granite. I immediately threw myself into cleaning the kitchen, unaware that I was washing and putting away the waffle batter before the au pair had a chance to finish making the batch until it was too late. I wiped off the granite and then stood there in front of my children with a sponge, determinedly catching the syrup drips just as they landed on the counter. I caught Samantha giving me an odd look, and the twins were staring at me as well, so I threw the sponge into the sink and moved on.

I spent the better part of the afternoon digging a shrub out of the front yard that had suddenly become unbearable. Miranda came out eventually to ask if she could stay over at a friend's house tonight, and for some reason the conversation turned into a lecture about the dangers of the pornography industry and its effects on the rising generation. After my rant I found her looking at my strangely, so I gave her permission to go and decided that I needed to hit the gym and clear my head.

It hasn't helped. My treadmill offers a window view of the street below, and I keep having to push aside the intense desire to go out and empty a trash can that I can see has overflowed. "I'm losing it," I mutter to myself as I slow down my pace to cool off.

A fresh white towel appears in front of me and I turn to see the smooth smile of James, the new fitness instructor with the uncanny knack of bumping into me every time I come in for a workout. I shake my head, smile and remove my headphones.

"Feeling better?" he begins, his eyes gazing deeply into my face. He is standing so close to me that I can see the flawlessness of his skin, a gorgeous chocolatey brown. "I thought about coming over to show you a new technique, but you were so intent on your run that I could tell you just needed to keep going."

"A little bit," I reply, dabbing my face with the towel. "I just had some things to work through, I guess." I look away, feeling a bit self-conscious that he had noticed so much about me.

"Anything I can do to help?" he offers, tilting his head to the side a bit. I watch him for a moment, the relaxed lines of his body, a teasing glint in his eye. There is an openness about him that is very disarming. "I'm just getting off the clock and was going to hit this great little sushi place down the street. Come with me."

"Thank you, no, James," I respond quickly, ignoring the ravenous feeling in my stomach that awoke at his suggestion. I realize that I haven't really eaten anything all day. But I'm also fully aware of my potential to attract men, and I'm not new to giving them the brush-off if they get too forward.

"Please, Vanessa?" he turns his head down towards me. "I could use the company. I'm new enough here that I have a lot of time to myself, and I definitely prefer people. Besides," he adds, "I'm a really great listener."

I consider him for a moment longer. Sushi does seem harmless, and maybe something out of the ordinary is exactly what I need to pull myself out of this funk. I sigh and reply, "Why not? I really am starving."

His face lights up and he grins down at me. "I like it! I'll meet you at reception in twenty?"

We make our way to the locker rooms and go our separate ways. As I shower and dress I reconsider my decision, wondering if I should come up with some excuse to avoid James. But I recognize that a part of me is really craving some attention right now—desperate for it, actually. Maybe he can help me through it, to figure myself out. And it is just dinner. I feel a pleasant anticipation, a welcome change from the agitation I felt earlier. I decide to treat myself to something unexpected, and walk out the door confidently to meet James.

❧

I wake slowly, inhaling a sort of masculine sweetness. The cotton pillowcase feels unfamiliar against my cheek. I suddenly freeze and my eyes snap open, adjusting to the darkness of my surroundings. I focus on the gentle rise and fall of the form next to me, slowly returning to the realization that the bare chest beside me belongs to James.

I close my eyes tightly and wait a moment to clear my head, hoping desperately that this is some strange dream. I can feel the aftertaste of the cheap alcohol on the roof of my mouth, feel the sheet pressed against my naked breasts, and I remember.

The dinner was nothing, really, and it was everything at the same time. I sat there with this man who I barely knew, and we talked and ate together for hours. He heard me. He was interested in me. In my work, in my family, my life—he was so engaging, asking questions and then listening for the answers. He made me laugh, even at myself. James wasn't looking for perfection, and he seemed genuinely entranced by me, my ambition, my successes. I found myself opening up to him in ways that I never could have with Michael.

It wasn't surprising or uncomfortable when I looked down and noticed his hand stroking my wrist, my palm, even tracing the outline of my wedding ring. I drank plenty, and by the time he asked me to come to his apartment I had long since made the choice to go.

James was as attentive with his lovemaking as he was with his listening, worshipping my body with a gentle confidence. I allowed myself to get lost in his touch, the firmness of his body, my mind so weary of the pain of my life that the present moment seemed the only thing that mattered.

And now here I am, lying next to him, listening to the hum of the ceiling fan in his room and the sounds of the city outside. I find my phone and check the time—3:27. Using the light from my phone to see in the darkness, I gather up my clothes and get dressed.

I consider leaving a note or waking him before I leave, but then realize that I have nothing to say.

The drive home goes by quickly in the quiet traffic of the early morning, and soon I have arrived at the dark silhouette of the house. I decide not to chance waking the kids by opening the garage door, parking in the driveway instead. As I make my way to the front door, I trip over something, catching myself awkwardly and hurting my wrist. It's the shovel that I had been using to remove the shrub yesterday afternoon. It seems a lifetime ago. I pick myself up, insert the key into the front door and turn the handle, determined to reassume the identity of the person I was when I left for the gym just hours ago.

ABOUT THE AUTHOR

Sophia Casey is passionate about life-long learning evidenced by her more than twenty-five years in the learning and education field and creation of the *Ease & Flow Academy* for leaders. Sophia received her education at UCLA and Johns Hopkins and is a member of Delta Sigma Theta Sorority, Incorporated. She is a featured voice on Amazon Alexa, and has been featured in *SUCCESS* magazine, and interviewed on several radio programs including SiriusXM, WHUR (DC), WRNR (MD).

In 2017, Sophia faced a major crisis in her life that would forever change it. Her husband experienced a traumatic brain injury which sent her family into a whirlwind of challenges. Sophia found solace through journaling and subsequently created the very popular *Ease & Flow 31-Day Journal: A 31-Day Journal to Get Clear, Connected, and Courageous About Life*. The journal includes daily structures to help you focus on your most important tasks, move your goals forward, practice self-care, and practice gratitude.

Sophia's joys are traveling with her husband, spending time learning from her son, and fundraising to help eradicate breast cancer and eliminate hunger. Her vision is to travel the world speaking and sharing her *Leadership, Ownership & Accountability (LOA)* program, launching her television show and continuing to create products and services to help others fully embrace their power with ease and flow.

CPSIA information can be obtained
at www.ICGtesting.com
Printed in the USA
LVHW030832201020
669251LV00009B/591